TWAYNE'S WORLD AUTHORS SERIES

A Survey of the World's Literature

Sylvia E. Bowman, Indiana University
GENERAL EDITOR

GREECE

Mary P. Gianos, Detroit Institute of Technology
EDITOR

Elias Venezis

(*TWAS 74*)

TWAYNE'S WORLD AUTHORS SERIES (TWAS)

*The purpose of TWAS is to survey the major writers
—novelists, dramatists, historians, poets, philosophers,
and critics—of the nations of the world. Among the
national literatures covered are those of Australia,
Canada, China, Eastern Europe, France, Germany,
Greece, India, Italy, Japan, Latin America, New Zea-
land, Poland, Russia, Scandinavia, Spain, and the
African nations, as well as Hebrew, Yiddish, and
Latin Classical literatures. This survey is comple-
mented by Twayne's United States Authors Series
and English Authors Series.*

*The intent of each volume in these series is to present
a critical-analytical study of the works of the writer;
to include biographical and historical material that
may be necessary for understanding, appreciation,
and critical appraisal of the writer; and to present all
material in clear, concise English—but not to vitiate
the scholarly content of the work by doing so.*

Elias Venezis

By ALEXANDER KARANIKAS
and HELEN KARANIKAS

Twayne Publishers, Inc.   ::   New York

To Our Fathers
James Karagianes
and
Stephen Karanikas

889.3
M527K

Preface

The subject of our study, Elias Venezis, has made important contributions to the literary renaissance of modern Greece. The high
quality of Greek writing since 1900 has been evidenced in a
number of ways. One dramatic indication was the recent award
of the Nobel Prize in literature to the poet and diplomat George
Seferis. Another was the astonishing breakthrough to world prominence of Nikos Kazantzakis—novelist, poet, and philosopher, and
runner-up for the Nobel Prize shortly before his death in 1957.
A third sign of this renaissance has been the publication in English
and other languages of many great but relatively little-known
writers such as Kostis Palamas, Constantine Cavafy, Anghelos
Sikelianos, and Stratis Myrivilis. Our interest in the Twayne Greek
Authors Series stems from the hope that these and other names
will become familiar to ever larger audiences.

With such a prospect in mind we began to prepare this intro-
ductory book on the many works of Venezis. Among these volumes are at least five books, three novels and two collections of
short stories, which easily mark him as a world author. Europe,
happily, has already made this judgment; his works, taken as a
whole, are known in a dozen languages. The English–speaking
world has not yet responded, because only one novel and a few
stories have been translated. Hopefully, our study of Venezis may
help to eliminate this omission by inspiring further translations
of his work into English.

We have attempted to make clear, concise summaries of Venezis' works for the non-Greek reader. They are impressive in
volume; they intrigue by variety of action and character; they
interest by their wide scope of theme and idea. The more purely
journalistic writings (which for the sake of his art may be too
numerous) express a range of subject consistent with Venezis'
stature as a man of letters, as a member of the Academy of Athens,
and as a leader in the Greek National Theater.

We have also sought to evaluate briefly, through the comments of others as well as our own, the aesthetic quality of his works, primarily of his fiction. Venezis is certainly a good journalist, columnist, and reporter; but his strength at the level which primarily interests us—his status as a literary artist—exists mainly in his novels and short stories. To these works we have devoted the bulk of our scholarship and criticism.

We have provided biographical and historical background to make the literature itself more understandable and meaningful. Unfortunately, only a minimum of formal criticism has been devoted to Venezis; most of the comments about his work are in the form of reviews which, although helpful to his reputation, do little or nothing to explain his artistic achievement. We have tried, within the limitations of our study, to provide this explanation.

In our endeavor we have to acknowledge the assistance of a number of people. We wish to thank the Oxford University Press and Phyllis K. Gomme for permission to quote from *Greece* by A. W. Gomme. Professor Mary P. Gianos, editor of the TWAS Greek Authors Series, has aided us on every occasion. We are indebted to Professor Kostis T. Argoe and the late Demetrios Michalaros, editor of *Athene*, for lending us necessary books and other materials. For similar reasons we thank Peter Pappas, George J. Drossos, Theano Pappazoglou Margaris, Kostas N. and Mary K. Scopates, George and Madeline Gountanis, all of Chicago, and Christos Gregoriou of Athens, Greece. Stephen Karanikas of Goffstown, N. H., was very helpful on the definition of colloquialisms. Professors John Curtis Johnson and Constantine Santas of the University of Illinois, Chicago Circle Campus, have been generous with their editorial counsel. We are most indebted to Elias Venezis for his gracious response to all our queries.

ALEXANDER KARANIKAS
HELEN KARANIKAS

Contents

Chronology

1904   Born in Aivali (Greek name: Kithonia), Turkey, on March 4, as Elias Mellos-Venezis.

1909– Attended the Demotic School in Aivali.
1912

1914   Family of Venezis fled to island of Mytilene to escape Turkish persecution. He attended the Gymnasium there from 1914 to 1918. After the Armistice his family returned to Aivali.

1921   Graduated from the Gymnasium in Aivali.

1921   War resumed between Greece and Turkey.

1922   Family of Venezis again fled from Turkey.

1922   In September of 1922 Venezis arrested by the Turks and placed in labor battalion.

1923   Venezis released from imprisonment in November.

1928   *Manolis Lekas,* short stories.

1931   *Number 31328,* the novel of his captivity.

1939   *Serenity (Yalini),* a novel.

1939   Venezis won both the National Prize for Literature and the Award of the Academy of Athens.

1941   *The Aegean,* short stories.

1943   *Beyond the Aegean (Aeoliki Yi),* a novel.

1943   Venezis arrested by the Nazis and condemned to death. Released shortly after a great public protest.

1944   *Winds (Anemoi),* short stories.

1946   *Block C,* a play.

1946   *Wartime (Ora Polemou),* short stories.

1949   Venezis invited for a three-month visit to the United States by the State Department under provisions of the Smith-Mundt Act furthering cultural exchange.

1950   *Autumn in Italy,* a travelogue.

1950   *Exodus,* a novel.

1952   *Archbishop Damaskinos,* a history.
1954   *The Defeated (Oi Nikemenoi),* short stories.
1955   *America (Amerikanikoi Yi),* a travelogue.
1955   *Chronicle of the Bank of Greece,* a history.
1956   *The Ocean (Okeanos),* a novel.
1957   Venezis elected to membership in the Academy of Athens. Retired from his executive position with the Bank of Greece. Became a director of the Greek National Theater.
1959   Venezis created a Commander of the Order of George I by King Paul of the Hellenes.
1962   *The Argonauts,* a travelogue.

CHAPTER 1

The Catastrophe of 1922

I *Introduction*

ELIAS Venezis' significance as a modern Greek writer may be approached in various ways. He belongs, for example, to the powerful group which successfully established the demotic as the dominant language of Greek literature. Venezis, by his practice, helped to confirm the victories already won over the purists. The purpose of such demotic writers as Aristoteles Valaorites, Kostis Palamas, and Nikos Kazantzakis (to name but a few) was not merely to use the people's speech, but to refine and ennoble it by literary exercise. The campaign to dignify the demotic had more than literary implications. It defined the writer's attitude toward such dynamic subjects as the monarchy, the structure of society, and the meaning of life itself. To be demotic as an artist meant to go beyond the ancient glories, myths, and memories, most of them already embalmed in lovely verbal forms, and to strike out for new literary achievement, using the common language, even though this often employed words that the purists regarded as vulgar.

Venezis is also included in the Aeolian School of Greek writers who derive from Asia Minor.[1] Apart from Venezis, the most prominent writers of this school are Milton Kontoglou, Stratis Loukas, and Stratis Myrivilis. Venezis, however, occupies a most important place as the leading chronicler of the Catastrophe, the debacle which the Greeks suffered in Asia Minor in 1922. Others have also written on this subject, but Venezis did so outstandingly in his first major work, *Number 31328*. This narrative relates in very realistic terms the author's own experiences as a slave in the labor battalions organized by the Turks. The theme of social upheaval that is depicted here is to reappear both in short stories and in other novels.

Venezis is very effective in dramatizing the exodus, the refugees on the road, and the fate of individuals uprooted and at the mercy of chance. Death happens as casually as suffering, and suffering is everywhere. But if the evil, as in *Number 31328*, results from the deeds of a human enemy, Venezis does not urge the reader to hate this enemy. One never knows in this precarious life how soon it will be the enemy's turn to be the poor devil whose grief must demand our pity.

Venezis also figures in the literature of modern Greece as a member of the "generation of 1930," a group of twenty or more writers who came into prominence in or about that year.[2] The two books which qualified Venezis for inclusion were *Manolis Lekas* (1928), a collection of short stories, and *Number 31328*, which was published in 1931. Within this very vital group are the Nobel Prize winner George Seferis, George Theotokas, Stratis Myrivilis, and Nikephoros Vrettakos. They are not bound together by any ideological affinity; yet they do form an identifiable group, and no other such coterie has come as close as this one to dominating the Greek literature of our time.[3]

Elias Venezis is a genuine man of letters. He has produced in every major genre except poetry. Still quite prolific, he has published sixteen books and hundreds of articles in magazines and newspapers. The wide range of interest in the journalistic articles shows his curiosity and sophistication. Of the sixteen books, five are novels; and three of them, *Number 31328*, *Serenity*, and *Beyond the Aegean* are undoubted masterpieces. Next in literary importance are his five collections of short stories. They begin with his very first book, *Manolis Lekas*, and end, as of this date, with *The Defeated*.

Venezis has also written several radio dramas. His one full length play, *Block C* (1946), reflects the agonizing days of his imprisonment and near execution by the Germans in October, 1943. The play survived its initial and disappointing performance by the National Theater and has since enjoyed regular production in the Greek provinces and on Cyprus.[4] *Block C* is an important part of his extensive literary reaction to the Second World War; and war, as we shall see, is one of his major themes.

In the five remaining books Venezis emerges as a traveler and historian. His three travelogues prove once again that this genre is popular in Greece. Some of the best writing of Nikos Kazantzakis, for example, is in his books of travel, such as *Japan: China*, a lively record of his adventures in the Orient.[5] In this category

Venezis wrote *Autumn in Italy, America,* and *The Argonauts.* Besides depicting the urbane tourist making visits to exciting places, these books reveal deeper aspects of his thought which have a bearing on his more significant fiction.

Both in 1952 and in 1955 Venezis published histories, *Archbishop Damaskinos* and *Chronicle of the Bank of Greece.* The term "chronicle" may best describe them since they are not based on the kind of scholarly research which we associate with today's historiography. The former book documents the activities of the Archbishop of Athens during the German Occupation, from the time he assumed the ecclesiastical throne on June 6, 1941, until the day of liberation, October 12, 1944. The latter book, which documents the history of the Bank, reflects the author's lifelong career as one of its employees. (Perhaps no other regular bank employee in the world has written more novels, short stories, and articles than he.) When Venezis retired in 1957, he held the title of Assistant Director. In the same year he received the highest honor his country can bestow upon an author: election to the Academy of Athens.[6] For several years he has been Director of the National Theater.

Despite his renown in Greece, Venezis has enjoyed but a meager reputation in England and in the United States. Only one of his books has to this date been translated into English; it is *Beyond the Aegean,* called *Aeolia* in the separately translated edition published in England. He is more widely known on the continent. *Beyond the Aegean* has been translated into nine languages, *Number 31328* into three, and *Exodus* into two. His works have been well received. The reason is clear: in his writings he exhibits a generally high level of talent. He has a wide emotional and intellectual capacity, and he gives of it with ample generosity. In his respect for art and love for mankind, Venezis is a faithful exponent of the best in Hellenism.

II *Historical Background*

The region of his birth and youth has greatly influenced the creative works of Venezis. He was born on March 4, 1904, in Aivali, Turkey, in the fabled Land of Quinces, not far from the equally fabled port of Smyrna. Venezis cannot forget that these were once Greek lands; they were Greek from time immemorial, at least from the days of ancient Troy. Closer at hand were the mountains of the Kimindenia. It was here, on his grandfather's spacious estate, that the young Elias lived the events he so movingly dramatized in *Beyond the Aegean*. What the island of Mytilene was to Stratis Myrivilis, what Crete was to Nikos Kazantzakis, this region of Anatolia, "my lost Aeolia," was to Elias Venezis.

His father, Michael Mellos-Venezis, belonged to what in England would be called the landed gentry. His mother, Vasiliki, was a girl from the Bibelas family; and it is her father who emerges as an epic and legendary character in *Beyond the Aegean*. In his preface to the American edition Lawrence Durrell states that the novel evokes another Garden of Eden, and it ends with another kind of Fall: the destruction of a boy's pastoral idyll by the First World War. The idyll in time would have withered away in any case for other and more gentle reasons; but the collapse came harshly for Venezis, with the Turks joining the Central Powers and quickly resorting to violence of a kind that can only baffle and sadden a ten-year-old boy.

For the duration of the war the Venezis family lived on the Greek island of Mytilene, away from their holdings in Asia Minor. The education of Venezis reflects this disruption. From 1909 to 1912 he attended the Demotic School in Aivali.[7] However, from 1914 to 1918 he attended the Gymnasium at Mytilene. When his family returned to Turkey after the Armistice, he attended the Gymnasium of Aivali and graduated in 1921. The very next year came the second great disruption, the Catastrophe of 1922. This time it resulted in the family's permanent expulsion from Anatolia. Venezis took his imperishable memories into exile.

His departure from the land of his birth was delayed by imprisonment in September, 1922. Until November of the following year, while his family found refuge in Greece, Venezis suffered what amounted to slavery in labor battalions dispatched eastward far into Turkey. These tragic months are graphically described in *Number 31328*. For a fuller understanding of this masterpiece of realism it is necessary to give a brief summary of what the Greeks still regard as the Catastrophe—the defeat of their armies in Asia Minor and the subsequent exchange of populations between Greece and Turkey.

Even after more than forty years the Greek mind has not fully recovered from the trauma. This is especially true of those ultranationalists who still dream of creating a Greater Greece at the expense of Greece's neighbors, primarily Turkey. They are obsessed with the idea that "We almost made it—and then came the Catastrophe." Greece had been ceded the Smyrna district in Asia Minor by the Treaty of Sèvres following World War I. But this important concession by Turkey apparently did not satisfy the revanchist Royalist Government which came to power in 1920 after the electoral defeat of Eleftherios Venizelos.

A British historian, A. W. Gomme, aptly summarizes the events that followed.[8] The government that replaced Venizelos did more than assume its commitments in the Smyrna district. It decided immediately that the forces of Mustapha Kemal, the leader who was rebuilding Turkey, had to be destroyed. Greece attacked without allies; indeed, Italy and France openly helped Turkey. "In the spring of 1921 the Greek forces advanced and were successful in several actions against the enemy rearguards, driving them back into the interior. In August they advanced further, as far as the Sakharia River, less than sixty miles from Ankara. But there Kemal was ready for them." [9] The military advantages were all on Kemal's side; the result was a Greek defeat.

The proud royalists and their king had sunk very low. Worse than this: the efficiency of the troops in Asia Minor had already been weakened by the dismissal of prominent Venizelists among the officers and the appointment of others for political or personal reasons; and in consequence of a growing discontent in the army after the defeat of the Sakharia, morale grew worse. The army was kept in the highlands throughout the severe winter of 1921–22 without adequate food or clothing, for they were still far from their base and supply was ill organized. Worst of all, everybody at home was losing confidence in the outcome. The pathetic journeyings of Gounares [the Greek Premier] and others in search of money and equipment did nothing to restore confidence, and by the spring the newspapers were hinting or saying that Smyrna was not worth fighting for, and of course blaming Venizelos for the policy which had landed them there. Such depressing matter was the only reading for the troops who for a year, while Kemal was biding his time, were kept inactive, discouraged, ill-fed and ill-equipped, partly disorganized, in a hostile country. No wonder that when Kemal did attack, at the end of August 1922, they broke and fled. The disaster was complete; they were driven back to Smyrna, more and more disorganized as they retired and losing all their equipment, and then out of Smyrna itself. Only the ability of the Greek fleet and merchant marine to rescue both them and many of the Greek civil population from off the shore and to defend the islands prevented the capture of the entire army; and only the presence of forces to the north and in Thrace, which could threaten a counter-attack, saved the country from the worst consequences of the defeat. It was a sorry spectacle only two years after the triumph of 1920, a triumph due to all the hard work and courageous fighting of the previous ten years.[10]

III *The Literary Beginning*

The historic disorder chronicled by Gomme and many others is deeply reflected in the work of Venezis. *Number 31328*, his first novel, depicts the aftermath of defeat as it struck the author himself. In general, Venezis conceives of the artist's role in the classical manner; the writer not only helps to engineer the human soul towards its ideal form but also to establish the broader values leading to moral and social order. What happens to people in their manifold predicaments (to which their *moira* or *kismet* often resigns them) becomes the substance of his fiction. The title story of his first collection of short stories, *Manolis Lekas*, is no exception.[11] The character of Manolis is more tragic than most others because he does resist his destiny. It is a remarkable tale, also, because Venezis was only twenty-four when he wrote it. "Manolis Lekas" reappears in the author's third book of short stories, *Winds*. Like his other early masterpiece, *Number 31328*, it is derived from his boyhood experiences in Asia Minor.

"Manolis Lekas" takes place in Aivali, the author's birthplace, in the street of Hagia Triada (Holy Trinity). The name of the street may be regarded as ironic; it suggests Christian salvation, yet the grimmest kind of blind fate prevails. If there is any divine providence here, it is all dire and malevolent. Manolis once belonged to the smuggling crew of Captain Stellaras. A simple man, he has to drink himself into a stupor before he can seek the opinion of his wife, Angelica. His manly pride demands that he be solely responsible for all decisions, that he not depend upon a woman for advice. His wife girds herself for the beating she must suffer at his hands, knowing that she must pay dearly for stating her opinion.

The problem at hand is whether Christos, their youngest son, should go to sea in the smuggling ships. The very idea horrifies Angelica. Her second son, Andreas, is already a smuggler and is constantly in great danger. In his later novel, *Beyond the Aegean*, Venezis romanticizes the lives of smugglers and makes their leaders ethnic heroes at odds with the Turkish overlords. In "Manolis Lekas," however, the illegal activity looms as threat and domestic tragedy. It must be resisted, for it can take and destroy another son.

Angelica's eldest, Aristides, is an idiot. Not only was he born an epileptic, but he was also beaten on the head with an iron rod by his drunkenly enraged father. Courageous in every other respect, Manolis cowardly refuses to authorize the necessary operation. The head wound closes but the child's eyes grow blank and colorless, and the great bald head seems monstrous on the small body. Having lost two sons, one to idiocy and the other to the smugglers, Angelica clings to Christos, the youngest. Though Manolis essentially agrees with his wife that the boy should not join the smugglers, he wants no one to suspect that he fears for his son.

He beats Angelica then goes to the forest to purge himself of his guilt. After he tries to help a neighbor's wife, who is beaten savagely for infidelity by her aged husband, Manolis questions his own actions. Returning home, he asks Angelica if she hates him for beating her. "No," she replies, "I cannot hate you. You are my husband. But please don't hit me hard. I am growing older now, and I can no longer bear the blows" (p. 141). Manolis seems constantly to battle with himself and the scheme of things. He tries to change himself and the destiny of his sons.

The smuggler son, Andreas, has just escaped death on Captain Stellaras' vessel when the Turkish coast guard gunned down the captain. Andreas says that when it is one's time to die, he does; he asks his mother which of her three sons is most secure. Is it the smuggler, or Christos, or Aristides the idiot, for whose death she prays? Although she denies that she prays for the death of Aristides, the reader learns that she indeed does ask God to end his suffering. But she also prays for the safety of the two other boys, especially for the youngest son Christos, who finally does not go to sea.

On the first Monday of Lent, Selas, an informer for the Turks, comes to the village tavern. When Selas discovers that the actor who plays the bear in the traditional Lenten Monday play is sick, he suggests that Aristides play the role. "Lekas won't mind," he says contemptuously. "He'll be happy to see the play" (p. 150). Manolis, restraining his anger, agrees. However, as the sorry ineptness of Aristides becomes clear, Manolis grows furious. He in-

sanely stabs a horse that panics and runs away. Then he begins
whipping the demented boy because he is fit for nothing, not even
to play the part of a bear. He insults Selas. Finally, in fury, he
goes to the forest to cool off.

The annual stone fight between the upper part of Aivali and the
lower part begins. All the hatred between the two sections is
stored for that day, then it explodes in the stone fight. Blood flows
readily and sometimes serious wounds are sustained. Quite often,
when the children's stone fight ends, the men take to venting their
rage with guns.

Christos Lekas and his youthful companions take part in the
violent stone fight. Aristides is allowed to tag along. Just as Manolis, the father, emerges from the wilderness becalmed, a man
running toward the town cries out to him, "One of the Lekas sons
is hurt!" Manolis rushes to his house hoping to find Aristides hurt.
Instead it is Christos. He lies dead with a small red hole just over
his heart. Manolis feels the hole and then caresses the boy's face
with his bloody fingers.

Venezis in this and in other stories is at his best in representing
the grimness of Greek village life. The only certainty, what the
people can count on, is bleak and tragic: the uncertainty engen-
dered by natural forces, by the Turks, and by the hatreds among
the Greeks themselves. Manolis Lekas cannot change the way he
is, his make-up, despite the fact that he pities the wife whom he
beats and suffers guilt for Aristides' idiocy. The course of events,
too, is unchangeable, as if a curse long ago fastened upon man
must slowly unfold to the grief of its victims. In this aspect of
their lives Manolis and Angelica are the heirs of Oedipus. Although not of noble birth, and though their griefs cause no great
ripples, yet like Oedipus they struggle against fate and lose. And
like Oedipus they display inner flaws, especially the intemperance
of Manolis, that tend to drag them toward defeat. We fear for
their debacle before it happens because we sense it to be inherent
in their nature, and pity them after it has occurred. The story
"Manolis Lekas" is a domestic tragedy brought on in large measure by one man's lack of self-control.

The novel *Number 31328*, on the other hand, represents the tragedy of thousands brought on by a historic defeat of a people in
the great Catastrophe.[12] It is the leading epic of the modern Greek
disaster.

IV   Number 31328

The family of Elias Venezis lost everything in the disaster; indeed, they were lucky to have escaped with their lives. Before their forced evacuation, Elias, then a youth of eighteen, was taken prisoner by the Turks and marched eastward to an unknown destination. If we are to accept Durrell's analogy, the Fall had occurred, Eden had been lost, and suffering had commenced. If the sin were that of pride, then the guilt lay ultimately with the politicians in Athens who were not satisfied with the gains made by Greece in the peace treaties, but who wanted to conquer Turkey entirely. After the defeat, only Elias went east of their Eden; the rest of his family went west, to sanctuary in Greece. And for more than a year, while he worked deep in Anatolia, Elias was unaware of their fate.

Number 31328 begins in October, 1922. In the sweetness of the Anatolian autumn the women, children, and aged of Aivali are disembarking for Greece. The men from eighteen to forty-five must remain to work in the labor battalions. Elias, concealed in a storeroom in his own house, watches the departure of the third ship. He sees distressing farewells. He also sees the humiliation of Lelekas, a one-eyed consumptive violinist, who is made to play from a high rock off which he tumbles. The next day a rumor spreads that the Turks have slaughtered the first shipment on the plain of St. George. News of the atrocity causes many people to go into hiding. A Greek who tries to bribe a Turkish sentry is killed on the spot. Elias, hearing of these events, silently ponders his fate.

Gradually the Venezis household empties. Elias cannot remain for long in the dark bin with its tiny window opening to the street. At night the rats scurry about and frighten him; he complains to his parents for not having brought him up to be unafraid of them. As the danger of detection grows, the family decides that Elias must surrender voluntarily to the Turks. The decision shakes the boy, but it has to be.

Elias is prepared for departure. During the last night at home, he huddles in the bin. He watches the Turkish patrols outside, hears the boat horns in the bay, and listens to the rats romping in the cellar. After a while his worried mother comes to keep vigil with him, to talk and to pray. "Much later," writes Venezis, "when she thought I had fallen asleep, I heard her begin to murmur to herself, as if she were speaking with God." [13]

In the jail where Elias goes, the cellar of a house, the Turks have crowded about forty men and three horses. The jail smells. It contains mainly Greek seafarers, men bronzed by the sun and wind; the author describes several of these men and gives their history and their fate. The nights in jail are full of musty air, snores, and moans inside, with tramping feet and other ominous sounds outside. By the third night, Elias learns that Aivali is almost empty.

Just before the prisoners depart from Aivali, the Turks bring in the boy Argyris, for whom Elias's sister, Agape (Love), has great affection. The Turks also bring in the watch repairman, Nicola, with his wife and three year old son. Guarded by bayonets, the detachment of Greek prisoners leaves Aivali. All day under the hot sun they walk on the road toward Agiasmat.

At the end of day Elias and Argyris feel lucky: they have remained alive. "We shall endure" begins to be a theme that is repeated throughout the book. The prisoners and their guards spend the night in a barn in Agiasmat. At about eleven the Turks remove the struggling woman. Three Turks overpower her outside while other prisoners try to calm Nicola, who is helpless to prevent the rape. Elias watches the deed. "Comrade, it is not a shame," one of the Greeks tells Nicola. "We can all affirm one day that you were powerless to do anything" (p. 55).

Next morning the detachment, joined by a girl of about twenty, proceeds toward Pergamon. Elias and Argyris feel sorry for the two women who are so often raped; yet while the women last to satisfy the Turks, the boys will be relatively safe from perverted assault. New emotions beset Elias as they pass the region of the Kimindenia Mountains; in their peace and beauty he had spent the summers of his youth. He remembers his grandfather, who was buried that spring.

The day's journey, as Venezis relates it, becomes a grim recital of hardships and peril. The captives trudge through fields where thorns pierce their feet. They cross a swamp where typhus lurks; they eat grass; they boil in the sun. In a vineyard the column of prisoners pauses briefly while the Turks rape both Nicola's wife and the girl. Their cries fail to bring help. The prevailing thought now becomes, "They will not endure." As the detachment nears

Pergamon, Nicola's terror grows for another reason. Earlier in the war, when the Royal Greek Army overran the region, he had participated in bloody reprisals against the Turks. Pergamon means certain recognition and death for Nicola.

The hard journey resumes after dawn. Behind the mountain of Tsambioi, they find a Greek woman who has miscarried and has been left to die. Nothing is done for her. One of the captives drops because of an attack of dysentery, and the guards promptly kill him. Then they kill another captive. "We drew ahead and waited below for the soldiers who remained behind to finish him off to catch up with us. How good it was to sit! The corpses [the prisoners] breathed deeply, they gathered strength" (p. 71). On this day of death they reach the town of Pergamon where more death awaits; Nicola is readily recognized and seized.

To everyone's relief his wife and son, who has had to be carried a lot, remain behind as the captives move on. Added to the detachment, however, are a group of starving priests and two new girls, one of them practically a child. This makes no difference to the soldiers who rape the girls repeatedly during the day's march. On the following day, the little girl dies, bleeding badly. For Elias a more personal tragedy is the death of his friend Argyris. Several Turks looking for an escaped Armenian notice Argyris' gold tooth. In a grim bit of horse-play they hit the boy on the head with a hammer and drag his lifeless body off to one side.

Ragged and weary, the captives march eastward for several days until they reach Kirkagatz. There the Turks divide the prisoners according to trades. Because so many buildings were destroyed in the war, there is a critical need for masons. Elias volunteers to help build an oven for a bakery, though he knows nothing about masonry. With the first rains, the oven crumbles, yet he is not punished. On various jobs Elias becomes acquainted with the other slaves, both the good and the bad. There is the smart operator, Glaros, who claims he can do anything. There is also Zack, a pianist, who initially works with Elias in the woods cutting logs. He becomes the piano teacher for the colonel's daughter. However, in time the girl wants him for her lover. Infuriated when Zack refuses her, she cuts his face and has him sent back to the logs with Elias. Not long after, in the town of Bakir, Zack dies, presumably of pneumonia.

At Bakir Elias works in a warehouse along with the boy Yiannis,

who believes that his family embarked for safety in Greece. They
had not. In one of several instances of Turkish compassion for the
Greek slaves, a mother brings Elias warm bread and a quince.
Later, when he has an attack of fever, he receives quinine from a
doctor, who eventually finds employment for him as a translator.

In another phase of his enslavement, Elias and two others leave
by train for Aksar where he is placed among Turkish deserters
and malcontents. A week later, however, he goes to Magnissa
where he cheerfully receives the official proof of his identity, the
tin plate with the number 31328. Now he cannot be lost in the
postwar upheaval. The killing of Greeks has about ended, but
typhus still takes its regular toll, and the chronicle of sorrows continues. Leaving the army camp at Magnissa, Elias is put to work
in a vineyard on a distant estate. In a field nearby lie the skeletons
of some five hundred Greeks. Elias returns to Magnissa after a
month to find new jobs and to meet new arrivals from other labor
battalions. Before long, spring flowers begin to blossom. The captives are allowed to rest on Friday mornings, the Turkish sabbath.

Summer arrives. While some of the Greek slaves go even farther
eastward for more punishment, twenty high personages of the
Greek armed forces are permitted to return home to Greece. This
rank preferment generates hatred in Elias and the others. At the
camp the old Turkish guards also want to pack and go home.
When they request their freedom, they are beaten by their com-
manders. The fates of the guards and of the captives mingle: they
are all *foukarades*, poor devils, victims of forces beyond their control.

Elias learns of the forthcoming visit of an international fact-
finding delegation led by a Spaniard named Dellara. The commis-
sion's coming creates intense work for the slave laborers. In a
ravine near Sipulo, the skeletons of forty thousand victims of
Turkish brutality are still piled in the open. Elias and the others
must bury these skeletons to conceal them from Dellara's investigation. On the morning of the delegation's visit, the camp officials
stage an impressive review. The Greek captives, who are kept
out of sight, return to the camp late that evening.

In August the heat is intense, but the big exhausting jobs are
over. Elias and his comrades sit around more often and entertain
themselves with stories. The first anniversary of Elias's captivity
comes and goes. Turkish refugees repatriated from Greece in the

population exchange arrive in the camp. At first they are hostile to the prisoners, but their attitude changes when the Greeks give them food and play with their children. The Greeks and Turks alike, more and more at ease with each other, have been victims of a similar fate.

Events now rapidly draw to a conclusion. In November Elias receives his freedom. He is no longer a captive; he is no longer number 31328. Nor is he a boy who fears rats; he is a man. During the last night in the camp at Magnissa, he goes around bidding farewell to old friends. He stows away a dog to take with him. When Yiannis talks of rejoining his family, Elias tells him the truth about their loss. Together the two boys await the dawn in the dark of night, in the dark of their lives. Elias looks at the line on the horizon where the sun will soon rise. "Yes, in a little while" (p. 222).

V *Critical Evaluation*

Number 31328 firmly established Venezis both as a chronicler of the Catastrophe of 1922 and as a member of the literary "generation of 1930." The critic Andreas Karandonis believes it to be one of his immortal works.[14] Of all his books only *Beyond the Aegean* has enjoyed more foreign translation. *Number 31328* has appeared in French, Italian, and Portuguese. Other books in Greek have been inspired by the tragic events in Anatolia, notably *Story of a Prisoner* by Stratis Loukas.[15] Nevertheless, it is still *Number 31328* that most completely reflects the deeds and emotions of the historic defeat. Venezis provides a panorama, while Loukas is limited by the stratagem of his hero's assuming the identity of a Turk. Brilliant as Loukas' brief work is, it hardly begins to explore the magnitude of the tragedy.

In *Number 31328* the author employs several major themes that recur as underlying patterns in his novels and short stories. More significantly than in *Manolis Lekas*, Venezis emerges in this book as a poet of social disorder. He places people in collision with hostile forces that have spun out of control; his characters, most of them simple and earthy, act and react to a fate that is usually blind. A major concern of Venezis is the impact of war on the lives of such people. In later novels like *Serenity* and *Exodus* he movingly describes what it means to be a refugee, to be alienated from every comforting tradition one has known, to be cast into grim wastelands where one can merely grub, sicken, and die; or, only with very great difficulty, manage to take root.

Another theme, strongly visible in *Number 31328*, is the fate of those in the hands of the enemy. The relationship between Greek and Turk is very subtle; hate and love are historically intertwined. Because of the centuries of enslavement of the one by the other, strong bonds developed as complicated as those between the white and the Negro in the American South. An added problem is the difference in religion: the Greek is Christian, while the Turk is Moslem. Thus when a scholar mentions the theme, "in the hands of the enemy," he must be conscious of the fact that in *Number 31328* today's enemy was yesterday's respected neighbor and friend. Yet friend or not, once the sword was drawn, no two people ever fought with more envenomed ferocity than did the Greek and the Turk. They both employed an ethnic mystique of cruelty which verged on the genocidal. Venezis depicts death, torture, and evidence of man's inhumanity to man with the compassion of one who believes that all men are poor devils in the hands of a pitiless fate.

A further general theme in *Number 31328* is the anguish of uprooted masses on the move. The protagonist is often the mass itself, differentiated by strong, unusual, or typical characters whose main problem is elementary existence. In *Number 31328* the hero is the author himself, but the book is not about himself alone; he is the focal point of a group, a large group sharing a similar status, slavery, and a similar purpose, survival. They are "on the road," victims of many kinds of evil, most, but not all, caused by other human beings. Ironically enough, these events occur for Venezis in the land of his youth, in beloved Anatolia, in the Eden that has turned him out. This theme of expulsion gives the author many opportunities for characterization, drama, symbolism, and analogies with ancient myths. Furthermore, the extended period of slavery becomes for the youth of eighteen the transition to manhood, a theme of universal significance.

The critical commentaries on *Number 31328* reflect these and lesser themes. They estimate the book's importance as a social and historical document. They praise Venezis as a humanist who hates war and injustice. They also praise his talents as a writer and chronicler of savage events; they compare him with other European masters of disorder and debacle. The fact that these com-

mentaries on Venezis are primarily general and impressionistic indicates the need for further critical evaluation of his achievement.

Reprinted in the fourth Greek edition of *Number 31328* (1959)
are a dozen excerpts from typical reviews in the European press.
They refer to the French translation of the second edition that
Venezis had reworked in the summer of 1945. Among them are
comments by members of both the French and Belgian Acade-
mies. In the Prologue the author explained that he returned to the
story because of the new trials and misfortunes of Greece. Venezis
also stated what several reviewers had noted: the timelessness of
the book as a chronicle of terror, written after the first great war
but reflecting so well the suffering of the second. As Jean Blanzot
said in *Le Monde Française*, contemporary writing about the horrors of the concentration camps had its precedent, without doubt
also its masterpiece, in Venezis' *Number 31328*.[16]

Most of the European critics represented revealed a feeling of
great sympathy and friendship for the book, for the author, and
for Greece herself. "The same happened to us," wrote the Belgian
academician Henri Liebrecht, "and thus, the more our reading of
the book proceeded, the more did our own agony overwhelm us
and would not leave." [17] The Germans in their use of slave labor
matched and surpassed the earlier brutality of the Turks in Asia
Minor. An interesting thought was expressed by André Bay, who
wrote in *La Gazette des Lettres* that truly good books scorn con-
temporaneity, "and when they appear it is as if they were being
awaited by the status they had to assume." [18] Such was the case
with *Number 31328*. In trying to establish the importance of Venezis in world literature Marcel Arland in *Gavroche* compared him
with Knut Hamsun; Marcel Augagneur in *Mondes* compared him
with Maxim Gorky and suggested that *Number 31328* was another
Anabasis; and Pierre Fauchery, in *Actions*, compared it not only
with Xenophon's *Anabasis* but also with Tolstoy's *War and
Peace*.[19]

That the novel is so patently autobiographical impressed several reviewers. "Venezis lived the book before he wrote it," com-
mented Liebrecht. This fact invited estimates of the character of
Venezis as both protagonist of the story and author of the book.
Atrocities against the Greeks occur in *Number 31328*, but it is not
an atrocity tale calculated to arouse hatred of the Turk. Rather
the opposite. Ilo de Franceshi in *Revue de Monaco*, who found no

trace of bitterness, declared the book to be a powerful hymn for
the ability of man to love, to understand, to unite.[20] The lack of
malice toward the conqueror was noted also by Robert Levesque
in *Domaine Grec*. Although Venezis has no illusions about man,
he does not believe that evil alone rules the earth.[21] Other critics
also praised him as a lover of mankind, of life, and of universal
peace. His compassion comes through most clearly, as indicated in
Number 31328, when the Greek labor slaves sympathize with those
other poor devils, the Turkish guards, and when they play with
the children of the Turkish refugees from Greece.

A book capable of moving so many readers for so many reasons
cannot help but elicit praise for the more formal aspects of its
excellence. Its sense of organic unity stems not from a causal plot
(to superimpose one on reality would have risked being mere
artifice) but from the compelling reality itself: the hero's odyssey
into the perils of slavery and his search for freedom. "The whole
book," wrote the French academician Georges Lecompte, "reveals
the art of a great novelist." The characters, he said, are amazingly
wrought in relief; and the scenes succeed one another with a
rhythm which continually becomes faster.[22] Liebrecht, too, praised
its artistic quality. "The beginning of the book, the panting march
of the slaves, men and women, is a Dantesque vision." [23] He regarded it as a model narrative which moves with frugality and
richness of detail. One critic, Albert Maquet in *Forces Nouvelles*,
wrote on the difficult art of staging, of rendering through significant details the necessary rhythm of a narrative.[24] The language,
including the dialogue, was a prime example of demotic Greek.
Here and throughout his later work, it may be noted, Venezis
makes very effective use of the sentence fragment. He does so
usually for emphasis, repetition, and dramatic pause. In general,
his art depends on atmosphere and realism; only when he falters
does it depend on sentimentality and abstraction.

The random references above to the style of *Number 31328* do
not, of course, exhaust the range of critical comment. They do,
however, suggest the exceptional value of the book to the career
of Venezis. In the Prologue to the 1945 edition, Venezis rejects an
unnamed critic's stress on the book's alleged sublimity, on its having transcendental and metaphysical meanings that involve the
supreme suffering of the soul. Venezis speaks instead of the "hot
matter," the tortured flesh whose blood drowns the book's pages.

The book deals, not with the soul, but with the human heart that writhes in pain. Here there is no soul, in the religious sense; here there is no place for metaphysics. Only philosophers and writers of books say that spiritual pain surpasses the physical. "But if you go out and ask someone on whose back death has walked (our epoch makes it easy to find one, there are so many) you will find that no pain is deeper than that of a body being tortured." [25]

Number 31328, the author states, is a testament of such a pain. The critic Apostolos Sahinis calls it "a naked and unadorned chronicle of horrid and blood-splattered incidents in which the dominant element is the particular episode itself." [26] The novel is a sensitive young writer's personal account of what happened to him, and to thousands of other Greeks like him, in the Catastrophe of 1922. The Eden he had known as a boy was lost forever in the great upheaval. Two other great novels stem directly from Venezis' boyhood in Anatolia and its bitter aftermath—the exile of his family and of all Greeks from their ancestral home in the lovely land of Asia Minor.

CHAPTER 2

The Anatolian Memory

I *Introduction*

ALTHOUGH Venezis showed growing competence in the short stories written during the 1930's and after, it was in his novels that he found his greatest power. Reviewers who speculate in superlatives have trouble deciding whether *Serenity* or *Beyond the Aegean* is the better masterpiece. Both novels continue the preoccupation of Venezis with the loss of Anatolia and its aftermath. The first dramatizes the unhappy fate of a group of Anatolian refugees trying to root themselves in a Greek wasteland after their exile from Turkey.[1] Although now in their own homeland, they find neither the people nor the land friendly. They are still being victimized by a dark destiny.

The second novel documents in beautiful poetic language the idyllic boyhood of Venezis in the Kimindenia.[2] For this touching story he mixes autobiography and regional legendry to produce a hauntingly nostalgic work. Both *Serenity* and *Beyond the Aegean* are realistic, powerful, and imaginative. The romantic elements in the latter blend skillfully with the realism. Together with *Number 31328*, these novels form a trilogy that encompasses the before, the during, and the after of the Catastrophe of 1922. Few works in modern Greek literature are more impressive.

The first edition of *Serenity* (*Yalini* in Greek) was published in September, 1939, the month when the German juggernaut attacked Poland. The bitterness in the novel, reflecting an earlier tragedy, fits in easily with the new griefs, and new disasters, as nation after nation, including Greece, fell to the conqueror. Things as well as people, Venezis wrote in 1943, are subject alike to fate; it was the fate of *Serenity* to have its early being in war and not in peace—a fitting atmosphere for a book that is so much immersed in the tragic destiny of man.[3]

Venezis used the occasion of writing about his novel in the Prologue to the third edition to reflect upon the history of the Greeks.

The immediate past of Anatolian Greeks like himself conforms to this unhappy history in general; as he says, "We are a truly wounded, much-tyrannized, much-embittered people" (p. 13). His own youth differed from the more normal youth of those who are fortunate; they store up reserves of happiness to be relied upon when they grow up. But Venezis knew only deprivation and tears. He was one of those sad children who are forced to think before they are hardly able to feel.

The pain of the modern Greek is organic with the traditional suffering of his people, which extends back to ancient times. The physical nature of Greece contributes greatly to the human torment. The land is difficult and arid. Even the seas around the land are impoverished; thus the fisherman's life is also hard. Greece lacks the endless plains and big forests of other nations; she even seems to lack the blessing of God who could lessen man's toil if He wished. "Our olives," Venezis writes in his eloquent Prologue, "grow on ledges and naked mountains, and are watered more by our tears than by the rain from the clouds" (p. 13). His litany to the pain of Greece continues with references to the ancient inhabitants and their intimate relationship with their gods.

The ancients had the wisdom to know that pain, unless experienced on the hands and heart and in the blood, remains an empty conception. These ancestors brought their gods down from the heavens and established them on earth, on Mount Olympus, in order to involve them with human needs and sorrows. Thus, when the pagan Greeks implored their neighbors, the gods, to send rain, the gods understood the plea because they were experiencing the same drought; the gods saw what it meant for this difficult land to need water, when water was not forthcoming from the clouds. When the ancients implored the gods for wind to fill the sails of their caiques, and to make the vegetation fertile, they knew that if Zeus but moved on his throne he could see their hard faces and hear the anxious beating of their hearts.

Then the gods of Olympus departed, Venezis goes on, and were succeeded, in time, by the dark ages of Greek suffering during which one conqueror after another subjugated the nation. Death became a familiar figure among the people. Among their other duties, mothers kept burial shrouds in readiness for the family in their trunks. Drinking to intoxication, which among peoples of other nationalities reflects joy, is for the Greeks a libation to the

god of bitterness. With bleary eyes the Greeks dance and sing
tragic songs. From this land, from this history, the modern Greeks
derive; and it is from this climate, too, that the novel *Serenity*
comes, "one of the bitter books of our heritage" (p. 14). Yet this
bitterness does not mean pessimism. Rather it is a common discovery of all living organisms. They ask much from life, and life
more often than not gives little. The physically and spiritually
aged can get along with mere crumbs. Therefore the bitter are at
heart the most optimistic; because with them still remains the
privilege of loving, of believing in people and in life, the privilege
of chasing chimeras (p. 14). Thus Venezis himself, in his Prologue, prepares the reader for the bleak and even gothic events in
the novel he ironically named *Yalini* (*Serenity*).

From the lushness of their lost Anatolia the refugees reached
their official place of resettlement, a barren wasteland in the
southern tip of Attica, at Anavissos by the Saronikon Gulf, about
ten miles from the town of Sounion. It is here that the peace
which the refugees needed and sought meant, quite as much as
anything else, the peace of the grave.

II Serenity

Two smugglers of antiquities, digging for lost treasure, notice
far below them on the mountainside a procession they cannot recognize. They work for Mr. Green, a shadowy figure who buys
antiquities illegally and has told them of a lost statue he wants.
The time is July, 1923. The procession is that of refugees from
Anatolia arriving to claim land given them for resettlement. It is a
wasteland without water, cursed by the gods. On the seashore
below are salt works, a symbol of sterility and death. The two
natives of Anavissos fear their plans for stealing antiquities will
be frustrated if the refugees remain.

The scene shifts to the newcomers. Doctor Dimitri Venis, sixty
years old, and his much younger wife, Irene (ironically named for
peace), represent diverging attitudes toward the wasteland. He is
hopeful, but she despairs. Their bickering implies an unhappy relationship. Venis comes from Phocis, a town in Anatolia famous
for its roses. Symbolic of his faith in life is his dream of growing
roses in the dry soil of Anavissos. Irene had been a rich girl who
felt superior to all her young suitors; when her father went bank-
rupt, she married Doctor Venis out of desperation. Helen Glaros,

a former servant in their household, recalls the prophecy of an old crone who claimed that the marriage was wrong.

Doctor Venis is a good man, but old and ineffectual. Although he admires Napoleon, he himself has never performed a strong and noble deed. He and Irene have one child, Anna, who lives in Athens. She arrives in Anavissos later to find a brief love and a quick ugly death.

The Vlachs, local shepherds of Romanian origin who tend their herds nearby, question the Phocian refugees about their origins and intentions. "Who gave you this land?" they ask. "Only we can survive here. It is only to us that the land speaks. Leave, or you will perish" (p. 49). The Phocians fear the bearded Vlachs, but they cannot leave; they have no place to go. The Vlach shepherds curse them; they will fight the Phocians for this barren earth.

The refugee families select lots on which they envisage future vineyards and fields of grain. Glaros, Helen's husband, thinks differently. He knows their settlement is on the ruins of an ancient city, devastated by an earthquake. Some of the ruins lie submerged in the sea off shore. When Glaros speaks of finding antiquities on his lot, Helen demurs, but Doctor Venis gives him sympathetic understanding. Glaros plans to ask Mr. Green, so named because of the color of his eyes, about the value of the old rocks.

Green had arrived in the area in 1911 as a digger for an archaeological party; when the others left, he stayed to become a kind of ghost among the ruins. Although reputedly wealthy, he exploits the refugees by selling them goods. He has a mania for antiquities. Green wants to rent Glaros's lot for three months, at a high price, but Glaros refuses. Glaros dreams of even greater riches—he will find a lost god.

Autumn comes and still there is no rain. Glaros has not found his lost god. He argues with Helen, who reminds him that others have been getting their land ready for vines and wheat. On a spot chosen by a diviner, he now digs for water and, to his great astonishment, he finds a god—the marble statue of a youth, a "blind god." Helen is afraid of their treasure; they cover it with soil again until Glaros can decide what to do with it. He lies to Green about his discovery.

When they return home, their daughter Zampeta has news for them: Irene's sister, Maria, and Irene's daughter, Anna, have arrived. They go to the Venis home to greet the newcomers. Later,

when Helen returns home to a restless sleep, Glaros goes to the
field to stand guard over his blind god. On the way he encounters
Green, who seems to have been snooping around. After Green
goes away, Glaros digs up the statue to make sure it is still there.
He realizes that the statue must constantly be guarded; otherwise,
it will be stolen.

The next day he makes Helen watch at the digging while he
goes off to get information from Green. Clouds quickly form in
the sky. A heavy rain falls. Suddenly, a flood rushes upon Helen.
In panic she enters the swollen waters and is drowned. Mean-
while, Glaros has been watching the rain and thinking, ironically,
of its life-giving powers. Happily dreaming of the deal he expects
to make with Green for the blind god, Glaros whistles as he goes
home to receive the gruesome news. Not only is his wife dead, but
the god is also lost. The refugees from Phocis had been unaware
that the footpath to their land was actually a dry riverbed. The
Vlachs on the mountain above had changed the course of the
waters to flood and destroy the homes of the intruders.

Glaros now buys a boat in order to become a trader in goods for
the refugees. He calls it *Helen*, after his dead wife. Dimitri Venis
reads the log of the Arctic explorer Captain Scott, whose frozen
body was later found by Amundsen. Scott's story is symbolic: he
died during an epic deed, and he did so in a wasteland, two factors that closely involve Venis. His daughter Anna, restless for her
lover Andreas who is still away, goes with little Zampeta to the
boats at the port of Saint Nicholas seeking news of him. Anna
chases chimeras. To her, serenity means love.

From the boats at Saint Nicholas, Anna brings home the good
news, "The exiles are coming!" The Phocians drop everything to
prepare for their relatives. Anna Venis goes to Sophia, the mother
of her beloved Andreas, to share her joy and to help prepare his
clothes. Irene's sister, Maria, who is nearly blind, also lays out her
son's clothes. The exiles do come, but Angelo, Maria's son, is not
among them. In fact, he will never come. Dimitri Venis and the
others decide to conceal the truth from Maria.

With the coming of spring, Venis has planted his rose bushes,
and Glaros has taken a new wife, a young refugee from the mountains bordering Persia. Now her father carries earth to his son-in-
law's dooryard to plant a tree for shade, which for the old man
means serenity. Andreas and Anna frequent the nearby forest,

gathering kindling wood. They stop to talk with Venis about his roses. Will they take root? They wonder if the search for serenity is not another chimera. At home, Anna tells her bitter and doubting mother that the roses show signs of life. "That cannot be!" Irene shouts angrily. "You will see!"

A stranger named Haritos arrives on a boat that is to take salt to the Dodocanese Islands. He comes among the Phocians to seek his fortune. Glaros hires him to do odd jobs. One day, they journey to the nearby island of Aegina where they will exchange salt, which Glaros steals, for pitchers that he thinks will sell among the refugees. Also on the trip are Vasso, who fears the sea, and the young lovers, Andreas and Anna. During the war, the three had spent four years of their childhood on this island. Visiting their old house, they find Angelo's name still chalked on the wall.

Before going to the olive grove, a place they associate with love, they visit with Stathis, old and blind now, in whose bakery Andreas and Angelo had worked as youths. They speak sadly of the past and of lost friends. Stathis calls Anna the "betrothed" of Andreas, and she is moved by the error. Leaving him, they rush in youthful ecstacy toward the serenity of the olive trees. There Andreas takes her roughly, desperately.

In the meantime Glaros sells the salt and buys the pitchers. He is ready for the return to Anavissos, but Andreas and Anna have not appeared. He sends Haritos to fetch them, knowing where they are likely to be. Haritos comes upon them secretly and watches their act of love from start to finish. On the way home the young lovers sit wrapped in mutual serenity. Haritos, moody and silent, sits apart.

Back in the settlement, they find new excitement. A steamroller, driven by a young mechanic, is there. A road which is to be built will provide jobs for the Phocians. Glaros sees another chance to make money. He will fill his boat at night with dynamited fish and sell them to the monger at Cape Kolonis. He needs dynamite, but does not know how to get it.

Irene Venis still expects nothing and believes in nothing. For her, the land has become a prison from which she badly needs to escape. Old chimeras of romance haunt her. Spring begins to make the wasteland bloom, animals give birth, and the women are pregnant with children conceived in the new land. The roses of Dimitri Venis share in the fertility. Late one night, Irene wakes and furiously uproots the bushes. She then goes to the mechanic who operates the steamroller and begs him to take her away. They ride off in the dark.

In the morning her family thinks Irene has gone out for an early walk. Anna tells her father she is going to the road and beyond, to gather greens for him in a forest glen. "A trip for greens in the golden earth." There, in the forest, a dark destiny awaits her; the drifter Haritos chances to come upon her alone. He demands from her what she gave Andreas on Aegina. She resists; he rapes her, then bashes in her head with a rock. Thus on the same beautiful day the stubborn believer in life, Dimitri Venis, loses both his wife, Irene, and his pulsating daughter, Anna, and his rose bushes lie wilting in the sun. Glaros, who alone suspects the identity of the killer, forces Haritos to admit his grisly crime.

Before he leaves Anavissos to seek his fortune in another country, Andreas talks with Dimitri Venis. It is autumn, and he finds the old man again preparing his rose bushes. "There is only the earth," Venis tells the youth, "but nobody believes in it" (p. 233). Irene Venis returns home from her brief quixotic adventure to wear black for Anna.

III   A Critique of Serenity

The motif of serenity, of quietude and peace, suffuses the story of the refugees on the Saroniko. They have traveled far for sanctuary. The word in Greek is *yalini*, a melodious word that implies benevolence and well-being, a sense of emotional completeness and fulfillment. It exists in the earth itself as a calm acceptance of natural law, of the eternal cycle of birth, growth, and death. Among the uprooted Phocians in Anavissos the search for *yalini* takes various forms; most of them are rooted in the elemental needs of existence.

For the aged doctor, Dimitri Venis, *yalini* means the growing of roses—hardy symbols of beauty, love, and life—in the wasteland where both the dry soil and the salt-filled air are obstacles. For his daughter, Anna, herself in the bloom of youth, chaste and lovely, *yalini* means loving and marrying Andreas. They both feel this serenity when they consummate their love in their idyllic olive grove on Aegina. For the character of Glaros (whose name means "gull"), *yalini* is finding a lost god, a rare antiquity, and the riches and comforts the sale will bring.

Others make the search for *yalini* in different ways and in varying degrees of intensity. That each apparent success is snatched away from the recipient by a blind embittered fate constitutes the tragedy of the story. "Venezis believes in fate," writes the critic John Hatzinis in referring to *Serenity*.[4] He attributes to the leading characters an innocence of desire which smashes against the harshness of reality. That the protagonist, Dimitri Venis, remains unbroken in his faith constitutes the story's glimmer of hope that man can ultimately triumph. Unfortunately, in the given circumstances, it is the tragedy and the pain that loom invincible.

In the Prologue alluded to earlier, Venezis suggests one of the major themes of *Serenity:* the suffering of the Greek people. In *Number 31328* the suffering is caused by the specific enemy of the moment, the Turks who command the labor battalions. In *Serenity*, however, the suffering derives from the diffused fate of the refugees, actually beginning with the Catastrophe of 1922 and pursuing them into exile. Their enemy is not directly visible. He neither shouts orders nor curses nor brandishes a gun; but he is there, pervading both the landscape and the huts of the homeless. This malevolent fate hits some with devastating blows, and the hardest blow of all falls, ironically, on Dimitri Venis, who believes most ardently in life.

The sufferings which beset the Phocians at Anavissos occur under conditions of political freedom; they have been resettled in Greece, their own fatherland. Yet in truth they have never known their parentage; they are Greeks from Anatolia, from distant lands "beyond the Aegean." Their freedom now means little more than abandonment in a hostile environment, at the mercy of those other nomads, the Vlachs. The Phocians are thus free to slave anew, to sicken, to despair, and to die. The Anatolians had reason to feel, perhaps, a keener sense of eternal suffering than those Greeks who had been liberated and united. Their Greece was in Asia Minor (with communal memories going back to the victory over Troy), and except for those brief and unstable months when the Greek armies had pushed eastward beyond them, they had known only Turkish domination.

The theme of upheaval, of people being violently uprooted

from their homes, is very strong in Venezis and in other modern
Greek authors. At the beginning of *Serenity* the two smugglers of
antiquities look down from a considerable height and see, blurred
by distance, the slow movement of a strange caravan. They are
unexplained intruders who embody, for the smugglers, mystery
and menace. A similar intrusion of refugees from afar occurs in
The Greek Passion by Kazantzakis.[5] Also coming from somewhere in the east, these refugees, guided by a priest, are relegated
to a barren waste. Their human needs become an issue in the
nearby village of Lycovrissi where the Passion Play has suddenly
been transformed from myth to immediate reality. Whereas these
refugees are a means of realizing the main plot of *The Greek Passion,* of testing the faith of others, the refugees in *Serenity* are the
main plot: their lives constitute the book.

Another major use of the upheaval theme occurs in *Exodus,* a
later novel by Venezis depicting events during the German Occupation.[6] The entire action of *Exodus* is the movement south from
northern Greece of some outcasts who are trying to reach Athens,
a supposed haven. That this haven, unknown to them, smells of
death from famine only adds ironic and tragic depth to the perils
they face as they tramp and ride onward. Their struggle for survival has a more desperate quality than that of the refugees in
Serenity; all about them, ready to strike, are the Italians and Germans. Their presence has smashed all hope of *yalini* and stability.
The outcasts are quarry on the run; they are fugitives in their own
homeland, and the landscape that was beautiful yesterday has become, today, a prison of fear and death. Thus Venezis in his fiction reflects how the Greeks of his generation suffered the social
disorder that was their lot.

He also reflects the modern Greek author's preoccupation with
the relationship between time past and time present. The ruins of
antiquity are too visible to be ignored; the question remains, to
what literary use does Venezis put the past with its tangible re-
minders of civilizations that have perished? In *Serenity* we are
told that the Phocians have resettled in a region where a city once
stood; an earthquake allegedly convulsed the city and swallowed
its inhabitants. From caiques just offshore one can discern in the
depths the submerged columns and walls of the devastated buildings. We can read into this fact a precedent of doom for the Phocians: the Saroniko is a region with a curse upon it. Nature herself

had once vomited death and destruction here; nature again, through excess of both drought and water, brings sorrow to her victims. The episode in *Serenity* that most concretely involves the past with the present is Glaros's discovery of a lost god.

For a while it appears that Glaros, to the dismay of his wife, will fail to prepare his land for useful crops; instead he will chase chimeras in his questionable gamble for antiquities. His apparent success, when it comes, foils him in three decisive ways: first, the god brings about the drowning of his wife; second, its theft denies Glaros his riches; and third, according to Dimitri Venis, the statue is no god at all. The statute's blindness may be interpreted variously, but the most likely meaning, in direct line of the classical Greek tradition, is that fate and justice are often oblivious to man's aspirations. Glaros begins to rebuild his life on new foundations once the fever for antiquities has left him; he even refuses to seek vengeance on Mr. Green, whom he strongly suspects of being the thief of his god.

The novel *Exodus* makes even greater use of time past than does *Serenity*. For example, a modern Antigone in the same setting as the ancient myth defies authority (the Germans) and buries a brother who has been hanged for being in the resistance. Also, some crucial events occur on Mount Kithairon; by means of legends written on the walls of a cave there, Venezis evokes past happenings associated with the region. These events helped to shape the fate-ridden heritage of Greece. It was on Kithairon that the baby Oedipus was to have been left to die. Legends on the cave walls tell of other desperate visitations at other moments in the past.

The assorted characters of *Serenity* scramble for their meager happiness in a time-haunted environment where the odds are heavily stacked against them. Dimitri Venis has more than the wasteland to contend with; he has Irene, the disillusioned aristocrat, who scorns and thwarts him at every opportunity. "Never!" is her typical reaction to the prospect of roses in the dry earth. Her own paralysis of emotion makes her a dead weight, a drag on both her family and her friends. To her former servant, Helen Glaros, she cries, "Let him strive by himself," when told of Glaros's enthusiasm for finding a god. When the other refugees pray for rain, Irene glumly says, "May it never rain." Her pessimism is so unrelieved that it almost turns her into an abstract symbol. To her

aging husband Dimitri, she is the much younger wife who has
always found him inadequate; and when the roses do grow, despite her dire words, she violently yanks them up—as if she wishes
to force her own sterility upon a reawakening soil. Only when her
daughter Anna dies, when her romance with the mechanic ends,
and her new sin matches an old one of her sister Maria, does Irene
Venis finally arrive at serenity: the calm of a mourning mother,
resigned at last to her fate, who walks slowly, speaks softly, and
wears ceremonial black.

This calm, of course, is scant comfort for her bereaved husband
Dimitri. That he has consistently been a sensitive human being
informs the reader that his is the more acute sorrow for the loss of
Anna. Irene has returned and the roses will grow again; but Anna,
the real flower of his life, has gone forever. Dimitri can commiser-
ate at the same tragic level with his friend Glaros. Both men,
however, typify the firm and essentially optimistic belief of Venezis that man must strive no matter what the adversity. He has no
choice but to go on; he is fated to do so. For Dimitri, an old man,
there is still some time for roses, for serenity. For Glaros, a much
younger man, there is work to be done. He must attend to justice,
for he kept the killer Haritos in Anavissos by giving him work.
He has products to buy and sell, and a boat to navigate on the sea.
More than that, Glaros has a new wife in Vasso to help bring up
the children; and there are the children, one of whom is symbolically named Dawn.

Venezis reserves for Anna and Andreas the lyrical language of
love in the wasteland. She is old enough, sixteen, to understand
the manifold stringencies of their existence, including the tension
between her father and mother. By the same token she is young
enough to indulge in romantic imagination, to chase chimeras, to
bask in the sun, to be in love. For Anna the landscape is more
than rocks and dust, the sky more than salted air. Her mind romps
above and beyond the barren earth to dwell on romance. She
awaits her *pallikari*, her handsome Andreas, who will return soon
from the toils of Anatolia. With her young friend Zampeta she
climbs the cliff for a better view of the sea and the direction from
which Andreas will come. Unknown to her, however, the gods are
preparing a tragic destiny; her portion of serenity has a cruel dual-
ism: a moment of ecstatic love, then a savage and senseless death.

Without a doubt the dramatic high point in the novel is the

rape-murder of Anna Venis by the drifter, Haritos. The deed is all the more gothic and shocking because of the relative rarity of rape in Greek crime. Anna's entire romance seems blighted by the stark naturalism that governs the land; her desire is another kind of rose seeking growth among rocks. Andreas, when he does arrive, seems emotionally paralyzed as a result of his experiences in the labor battalions. His best friend Angelo is dead, and he must keep the secret from Angelo's mother. When Andreas finally takes Anna in the olive grove on Aegina, he does so violently, without tenderness—and it happens, by sheer chance, with the eyes of Haritos secretly upon them. Later, when Haritos finds Anna alone, he grossly demands from her what she willingly gave to Andreas. She fights back, and is killed when the rapist panics. Thus does the daughter of Dimitri and Irene Venis go from the *yalini* of love to the *yalini* of death.

Venezis has indeed written a bitter novel in *Serenity*. His dramatic method has been the pairing of opposites, making possible a continual undercutting of promising event. The very title is ironic. Every time a desire seems on the point of being realized, something bad happens to effect a tragedy. It is as if Venezis is dramatizing again, through vignettes of character, the great Catastrophe of 1922, in which the ironies of fate had worked overtime. Then, too, the prospects had at first seemed most promising, for the victorious Greek armies had almost reached Ankara in the heart of Turkey. But the seeming glory speedily turned into its opposite, into a defeat that still haunts the Greek imagination. In *Serenity* the refugees from that Catastrophe, now rooted upon barren land, must still live at the mercy of these ironies; they must still struggle and die before they can be secure in their haven.

IV   Beyond the Aegean

The third novel in what may be regarded as a trilogy, *Beyond the Aegean*, represents the Anatolian memory before it soured. After 1914, when the story ends, came World War I and the first exile of the Venezis family. This initial separation from their Anatolian home was followed a few years later by the Catastrophe and their permanent expulsion. The two novels already discussed dealt with the more immediate effects of this debacle: in the one, the pain of slave labor under the Turkish lash; in the other, the slower but also deadly corrosion of resettlement. Now, in *Beyond the Aegean,* the author reaches back into his youth to evoke, through an obvious labor of love, the memory of his lost Anatolia. It was not his loss alone, but that of every Greek in every refugee quarter on the mainland. Not all Greek refugees derived from the same landowning class to which the Venezis family belonged; yet whether rich or poor they were equally uprooted—they all had something precious to remember. After reading *Beyond the Aegean* one can return to the earlier works of Venezis with an even greater awareness of the Greek refugee's sorrow; and one can share with the author his lament for the stupidities and futilities of war. For it was war, and man's inhumanity to man, that wrenched Greek and Turk apart in their previously integrated Garden of Eden. It was nationalism and politics and religion and exploitation that not only made that Garden unstable but finally destroyed it altogether.

The structure of *Beyond the Aegean* comprises three parts: "The Discovery of the World," "Song of Awakening," and "Symphony of the World." Each part indicates a stage of growth in the knowledge of the protagonist—Elias Venezis himself as a boy from six to ten. He learns from both nature and man. The setting is not the family's home in the town of Aivali, as was the case at the beginning of *Number 31328,* but his grandfather's estate on the Kimindenia, a mountainous region northeast of Smyrna. There, in a lovely pastoral region, where the mythical past impinges heavily upon the present, the Venezis children spend their summers. In his Preface to the book Lawrence Durrell writes: "In Eden there was no time, but only a blessed continuum of happiness; this novel, with its skillful arrangement of moods and atmospheres, makes another Eden of the lost Anatolia." [7] Presented by the author in the first person, these moods reflect the legends and myths of the Kimindenia. They are based on real people, on their agonies and joys. Finally, they reflect the land and the imagination of one who knows that the land breathes and speaks and sings; and sometimes it moans and cries in the dark, whipped by chimeras for reasons impossible to explain. Although episodic, the novel is unified by these moods, by this point of view, and by a series of happenings that involve basic elements in a boy's growth: innocence, knowledge, wonder, loyalty, heroism, trust, understanding, and reflected sorrow.

Part One, "The Discovery of the World," begins, "My ancestors laboured hard on the land which lies below the Kimindenia, and by the time I was born a great part of the region belonged to our family." [8] At his grandfather's farm in the mountains the boy Elias (called Peter in the novel) spends his summers together with his mother and four sisters: Anthippi, Agape, Artemis, and Lena. The kind and wise grandmother is a refuge for the children in both calm and crisis. The grandfather, Jannako Bibelas, looms as an epic figure respected by brigand and Turk alike. Into this wild and beautiful region comes the sea-bred boy from Aivali. He misses the smell of the seaweed, but in time he learns "to love this land, rooted in unalterable peace" (p. 19).

The boy awakens to the mingled myth and reality of the land. The buildings on the estate face inward to a courtyard and are joined by a balcony. Only grandfather has a window, strongly grilled, that faces outward to the world. "The building somewhat resembled a monastery or a fortress, built entirely of the ancient stone of Sarmousak, because of the fear of brigands" (p. 3). Brigands infest the Kimindenia; they, too, are epic figures with a stern code of honor. Next to the children's nursery is the weapons room, the Yellow Room, filled with rifles and swords; and sometimes at night when jackals howl outside, the swords in the locked room awaken and sing. Venezis eloquently captures the mood of wonder when he writes, "The sounds of the forest and of the earth, of the deer passing, were all part of a strange music which sang of fairy tales and dreams, of children who rode on golden fish to find Princess Scarlet Slipper with her white dress and silver hair, whose gate is guarded by the Great Dragon" (pp. 5–6).

The Kimindenia is a land of magic, and some of the legendary heroes who walk upon it emerge in the nostalgic tales told to the children by Jannako Bibelas—like the time of the drought and the unexpected visit of Lazos the brigand, the day after the second girl, Ourania, was born. Lazos and his men arrive to collect a tribute from Jannako; they are moody and menacing as they drink and feast at the table. Suddenly, into "the atmosphere of wolves, of bullets and guns and the masculine smell of unwashed bodies came the incongruous feeble voice" of the newborn baby, Ourania, "supplicating for its life" (p. 17). Lazos asks, "What was that?" and Jannako tells him. The brigand is stricken with shame, speechless with anger at himself for being boorish and unmanly so close to the holy moment of birth, and the mother very ill. "Why

didn't you tell me about it, oulán?" he shouts (p. 17). Lazos rises
at last from the bench where he has lain transfixed, hands the little
black bag containing the tribute money to the old nurse who
tends the young mother, and says, "Tell her that Lazos gives it to
her for the dowry of her daughter" (p. 18). He and his men
mount their horses and disappear into the cold night.

The tale of Lazos is one of many the children hear in the
Kimindenia. They hear others, and some they do not have to hear
because the events happen before their eyes. For example, one
time the Great Dragon, the benevolent god of the forest, forgets
to feed the starving jackals and they descend in hordes upon the
fields of Jannako Bibelas. Their raids provide the boy Peter with
his first definition of war; it requires war to drive them off, at
night, with torches and drums and guns. "Falteringly, fearfully,"
Venezis writes, "we approached nearer to the meaning of the
cruel law of nature" (p. 28). Cruelty, however, is only one of
nature's moods. There are many more, like the case of old Uncle
Joseph, the expert grafter of fruit trees, who does not believe the
superstition that he who plants a walnut tree will die as soon as it
bears. But Artemis does believe, and she rushes to plant the walnut tree before Uncle Joseph can.

From the peasants in the fields the boy hears countless tales
about brigands and corsairs and ghosts and miracles of the saints.
"Our farm was on the artery of the great highway which joined
the shores of Aeolia with Pergamon, and from there led into the
heart of Anatolia. Thus we were familiar with the travelers on this
great road. There were Jews, Armenians, Turks, Christians, beggars, nobles, peddlers, the sick. They brought with them their destinies, their passions and miseries, their schemes and follies" (p.
50). When a "real traveler" arrives, the children fuss over him and
bribe him with milk and eggs; and they hear wondrous tales like
the two reproduced in the book.

The first concerns Ali, the Moslem camel driver, a member of
the tribe known as the Tsitmi. He spends his life searching for a
little camel with a white head. Once, he had owned the camel,
which he loved, but his wife had beguiled him into selling it.
Finding life without the camel intolerable, he left home on a for-
lorn search that will apparently never end. The second tale concerns Stephanos, the saddle maker—a propertied citizen who
scoffs at all wanderers, reads books, and is ashamed to admit his

occupation, thus invoking the superstition that once one "denies one's saddles" one permanently loses one's skill. Stephanos, as the story unwinds, is doomed to wander the earth in a futile search for perpetual motion.

Time passes, and the boy Peter grows to be ten. He now participates more directly in the events depicted. Now the children hear about ghosts from peasants who thoroughly believe in them: from Kosmas Levas, who blames a ghost for the failure of his life; and from the islander Manolis Liras, who sees the Gorgon, the spirit of the sea, to whom he has to say, "The great king lives, Alexander the Great lives!" (p. 93). Finally, there is the "hunter with the yellow stars" who tells Artemis, the oldest sister, about the strange and beautiful bird called the hoopoe. He also tells her about the Scottish girl of Greek lineage named Doris who is coming to marry the son of old Villaras, his employer. Doris has an important role in Part Two, "Song of Awakening," in which the boy gropes toward manhood. She generates a rivalry between Artemis, who is thirteen, and Peter. Artemis is jealous of Doris because of the latter's friendship with the young hunter. To Peter in a fit of anger Artemis says, "You will never be a hunter," but when he kills a weasel with his slingshot, she shouts "Wicked!" and strikes him. He strikes back.

In "Song of Awakening," the problems of Peter become more personal and more complicated. They mingle often with those of Artemis who is becoming a woman—awkward, fitful, unpredictable. Doris widens the scope of action to include the neighboring Villaras family, the greatest landowners in the region. "Leading the way came the horsemen of Antonas Pagidas, the foremost smugglers of Aivali, girded with cartridge belts and with their glittering rifles slung from their shoulders, their black fur caps adorned with gay colours" (p. 129). The newlyweds, Doris and her husband, are thus welcomed home. Behind them, a camel caravan bears their luggage. Later, as part of the welcoming festivities, the parents stage a truly Byzantine spectacle: two huge male camels fight almost to death over a female camel. Doris, the newcomer, says that she "liked it very much."

Just as her presence motivates Artemis to jealousy, so does it motivate Peter to heroism. For Artemis he killed a weasel with a slingshot; now he wants a gun to become a real hunter. He seeks to plunder an eagle's nest high on a dangerous cliff, so he may steal an eaglet as a gift for the beautiful bride from Scotland. He goes ahead one day in the face of a summer storm, reaches the nest, and is about to snatch the eaglet when the fierce mother eagle returns. Doris shoots and kills the bird just in time. When Artemis accosts the hunter to ask what happened, he replies, "Your brother wanted to go up to the eagle's nest, and my mistress killed the eagle. She did what no other woman in our country would have been able to do. If her aim had wavered an inch, she would have killed your brother" (p. 161). Thus by her beauty, her skill as a marksman, her knowledge of nature, and her love of the wild, Doris makes a quick entrance into the legendry of the Kimindenia. Her independent spirit contrasts sharply with that of the traditionalist women of the region.

Another crisis occurs when Villaras' hunter takes Doris to the wild boars' cave where he had previously gone with Artemis, his "little fawn." To this cave come the old boars when they want to die, and here Artemis and Peter keep their tortoises and lizards and eggs stolen from wild birds. Artemis follows to contest Doris's exploration of her sacred sanctuary. In an angry scene she hysterically tries to keep Doris out; but the hunter roughly pushes her aside, making her fall. In revenge, Artemis cuts the strap of Doris's saddle with her pocket knife. Nothing happens to Doris on the return. Something horrible, however, does happen soon to the young hunter. He is murdered by armed Turks, and with his death ends, on a somber note, the "song of awakening."

The third and last part of *Beyond the Aegean*, "Symphony of the World," opens with the gate to the estate closed because of the rising danger of war. The year is 1914. Most of this section concerns Antonas Pagidas, the leader of the Aivali smugglers. Venezis writes about them with pride in their manhood, in their nature as *pallikaria*.

They were reckless, abandoned souls, the passion for blood and danger burning in them like a demon. They gambled with death every day of their lives, attacking and being attacked. Death and fire were their playthings to be tossed about recklessly to give their life meaning, and to sweeten the hours when the demon was appeased and they could put up their swords. And yet no one could be more liberal, for no smuggler ever hoarded the gold in his countless store. They squandered it on fabulous orgies which lasted for days, they spent it on women, and distributed it to poor families. And so this foolhardy game kept a certain integrity, having no practical aim. As the game grew wilder and more irresistible, the dream of tranquillity became more elusive. Their swords never cooled, for peace came to them only in the grave. (p. 206)

The smugglers, who never pardon a thief but respect murderers, bring contraband tobacco of Aounia "from the regions of Balikesher" to sell in Aivali or ship abroad. Antonas Pagidas leads one gang. The opposing gang, the Koltziades, is led by another *pallikari*, Stratigos Garbis. Much of the final section involves their fate which, on a point of honor, compels them to engage in single combat. They respect and love each other, but one has to die.

This inner tragedy is brilliantly interwoven with the universal tragedy whose initial portents have begun to manifest themselves in the Kimindenia. The murder of the Villaras hunter is soon followed by other Turkish atrocities against the Christians; then come the pillage and massacre of whole villages and the consequent appearance of a familiar spectacle in the writings of Venezis: refugees on the road seeking a bitter haven. The children whose point of view has dominated the novel, and especially that of Peter, again turn passive, filled with awe and shock. Their idyll of adolescence has ended. Ahead lie the sorrows of upheaval and exile, begun with a rush to the sea, to the caiques and the ships, in order to escape the onrushing enemy.

So great is the honor among the smuggler chieftains that even the catastrophe of war is not sufficient reason for delay in settling the dispute that divides them. Antonas Pagidas has a younger brother Konstantin, frail and unworthy, on whom nevertheless he lavishes more indulgence than "to anyone else on earth" (p. 210). Due to a misunderstanding and to an altercation which is all the fault of Konstantin, he is killed by Stratigos Garbis who had once saved the life of Antonas Pagidas. Now, however, because of the blood which has been spilled in the death of his brother, Antonas must challenge his respected friend Garbis. The time and place are set in this dire message from Antonas to the rival chieftain: "You will tell Garbis that I shall kill him. I will meet him outside the farm of Jannako Bibelas on Tuesday, at the setting of the moon" (p. 212). The ritual of honor, barbaric, splendid, and sad, has to be resolved no matter what is happening to the universe. Before the fight, with Doris along, Antonas Pagidas and his smug-

glers distribute guns to the Greek villages in the region. She alone
does not know why these rough and bloody men are so solemn, or
why they tell stories of legendary deeds. The battle between Pagidas and Garbis will also become a legend. And at the appointed
hour, near the farm of Jannako Bibelas, with the children knowing about it, the two *pallikaria* fight. "Their knives flashed in the
darkness as they leapt at one another, groaning and choking. The
whispering trees stood silent, and the stars looked on, inclining
themselves long and intently over the earth" (p. 253). From the
bloody ground only Antonas Pagidas returns, with the heavy
knowledge that he has just slain his noble friend.

This inner and more personal tragedy occurs while the people's
exodus from their Anatolian homeland is already in progress.
Once the fight is over, and Stratigos Garbis has been buried under
the giant oak near the Bibelas gate, everyone's attention turns to
the greater peril: the approaching Turks. At the beach Antonas
Pagidas does not board the sloop taking his men and others to
safety. "He was going out alone to fight the horde which was about
to descend upon him. He would die, but there was no other course
for him. He was going to rejoin the friend he had killed" (p. 258).
Finally, the children of the Venezis family leave the Kimindenia,
leave Aivali, the land they love. They board a vessel which carries
their childhood dreams out to sea. Their grandfather, Jannako
Bibelas, salvages a handful of earth to remind them of their lost
Anatolia. In this memorial soil they will plant a sprig of basil. The
novel ends with the quiet lament: "Oh, land of my birth, Aeolia,
my native land. . . ."

V   *A Further Critique*

Much has already been noted about the structure and appeal of
Beyond the Aegean, of its division into three parts and its various
moods and meanings. This most poetic novel by Elias Venezis is
the best known of his works outside Greece. Much of the commentary on the book consists of praise for its author; very little of
it, unfortunately, attempts to help the reader understand either
the author or his book. What is regarded as *kritiki*, criticism, in
Greece is usually limited to impressionistic book reviews in which
the writer is more interested in displaying his own ideas than in
making a disciplined aesthetic analysis of the work at hand. The
ethnic and patriotic search for the Greek spirit, the Greek charac-

ter, and the Greek soul, important as that might be as an aspect of historical criticism, hardly begins to evaluate artistic achievement. The formalist and genre criticism inspired by *The Poetics* of Aristotle has very few practitioners in modern Greece. The tendency of critics is to make generalized comments, interesting in themselves, which explain the work as a social, psychological, or cultural phenomenon. The masculine giant of nationalism has not yet fully consummated a marriage with his delicate bride, aesthetics.

An intriguing but non-aesthetic judgment on *Beyond the Aegean*, for example, is that of Anghelos Sikelianos, the great demotic poet, who wrote the Prologue for the second edition in 1944. Regarding himself as a Dorian, a mainlander, he recalls how the cultural union of Doric and Ionic created the miracle that was the life, thought, and art of ancient Greece. Like the author Venezis, the Ionians also lived "beyond the Aegean," in lands and on islands off the lands that were later known as Anatolia, the "East." It was from the natural philosophy of Ionian thinkers like Thales and Heraclitus that the clear light of reason began to pervade the whole of Greece. In paying both them and Venezis tribute, Sikelianos writes, "Ionia has not vanished. Ionia lives." [9] One way it does so is through the spirit and art of Elias Venezis.

Lawrence Durrell evokes the past in a different way. There are two pasts in his Prologue to *Beyond the Aegean*: the immediate past of the Greek refugees and the old Greek heritage, remnants of which had survived in Anatolia. One visits the refugee quarter of any Greek city, Durrell states, and "hears snatches of old-fashioned Greek—fragments of Doric that were once carried up to the shores of the Black Sea, and that have now been washed down here to this barren littoral by the waters of history." [10] With a rich lyricism that betrays his own emotions, Durrell lists various details of the refugee's memory, a song that "speaks of Smyrna," the streets with "their huddled cafes," the "glass birdcages swinging in the honeyed summer air," the "bubble of the *narguilehs*," the "red *fezs* dotting the plaster walls. . . ." (p. *v*). The first past, then, is the lost Garden of Eden in Anatolia. The second leaps across the centuries to something far more primitive, to a lost heroic age that survives in the way of life depicted in *Beyond the Aegean*. Bits of this heroic past also survive, one may say, in other parts of Greece, notably Crete and Macedonia. Durrell, in suggesting this quality, writes of the book, "The world it describes is strangely archaic: it is nearer to the pastoral world of Hesiod and Homer than it is to our own." (p. *vi*). Thus both Durrell and Sikelianos establish Venezis at the deepest level of the Greek heritage—where the past reaches out to mold and motivate the present.

Pierre Amandry, who translated the text and wrote the Prologue for the French edition (*Terre Eolienne*, 1947), mentions the Greek past of western Asia Minor to render more poignant the characters and events of the novel. After the burning of Smyrna, the bloodiest episode in the Catastrophe of 1922, a million Anatolian Greeks left in the exchange of populations to crowd the refugee quarters cited by Durrell. Their ancestors were the Ionians who as early as 800 B.C. sent trading vessels westward to Gibraltar and northward to the headwaters of the Don. From then until 1922 the Greeks had had a continuous existence in Asia Minor. Amandry agrees with Sikelianos that the spirit of the heroic age relives in the work of Venezis. The French critic expresses his fascination with the characters, whom he divides into two categories: the simple honest lovers of the land, bonded with nature, and the outcasts beaten by misfortune, the smugglers and the madmen. With the first he associates the children, Peter and his four sisters, and what they learn from the Kimindenia. In defiance of the superstition about it, Artemis had planted a walnut tree; a few years later, Amandry notes, she did die and was buried on the island of Lesbos, where the Venezis family had retreated during the World War. The children are created with sensitivity, but without the sentimentality that could easily be the result of the cruelty and barbarism that they see. As for the romantic brigands, Lazos, Pagidas, and Garbis, Venezis loves to depict obsessed heroes driven by monomania and chimeras—such as Dimitri Venis in *Serenity* and his dream of roses. "The narration of *Beyond the Aegean*," Amandry writes, "is excellent, lively, and graphic." [11] And the stories the children hear, of folk heroes like Lazos and Pagidas, are myths of Anatolia woven by the artistry of Venezis into the fabric of their lives.

A novel so widely read has also been widely reviewed. On the inside cover of the sixth Greek edition, for instance, are excerpts from eleven reviews representing eight countries and various critics as far apart, geographically, as Professor Cedric Whitman of Harvard University and Hagar Olsson of Finland. These reviews and others like them indicate that *Beyond the Aegean* was received with universal praise. "You have surpassed yourself," the Greek critic John Hatzinis said upon meeting Venezis after the novel appeared. "The fear is that you will not be able to reach yourself again." [12] Professor Whitman writes that even with this one book Venezis rates as one of the greatest novelists of our time.[13] *The Times Literary Supplement* stresses the unforgettable characters, such as the hunter and the smugglers, and the way of life that was so soon to be gone. A German critic, Erhart Kästner, credits the world-wide success of the novel to its warm and tender treatment of youth, a universal theme. He urges his fellow men of letters to welcome the brilliant guest, Venezis, who has come to them through the book's translation.[14] M. A. Cavazzuti, writing in the *Quotidiano* of Rome, notes that this was the first Greek novel to be translated into Italian; this constituted an important step toward further understanding between the two nations.[15] The Finnish reviewer, Hagar Olsson, writes, "How happy we are when the books we read keep overflowing and flooding our hearts as we proceed in our reading." [16] Such a book, he says, is *Beyond the Aegean*, which made a sudden and exotic appearance before the Swedish-speaking public.

Although of limited value as aesthetic criticism, these reviews interest the scholar because they indicate the nature and scope of Venezis' literary reputation. No other single book has done more to make his reputation illustrious and worldwide. Written during the manifold pains of war, *Beyond the Aegean* is the creative result of a backward glance, saturated with feeling, to a lost youth, a lost peace, a lost Garden of Eden. In the two collections of short stories that appeared during the same fertile wartime period, *The Aegean* in 1941 and *Winds* in 1944, Venezis weaves a varied pattern of theme and event based on much of the same rich material. The best of the stories have the same fidelity to truth and the same beauty of expression.

CHAPTER 3

The Earlier Short Stories

I The Aegean

TURNING from his first novels to another genre in which Venezis excels, the short story, one finds a rich variety of setting, action, character, and theme. The appearance of his five collections of short stories spans the years from 1928 to 1954. The publication of some seventy stories is a rather prodigious effort in view of all his other books and articles. The best of these stories, in our judgment, are those summarized here. The best of the five books themselves are *The Aegean* (1941) and *Winds* (1944).[1] Most of the tales and stories here have the power that results from careful and complete realization; some begin to exhibit the sketchiness and excessive reliance on theme that often mar the stories written after the war.

His short fiction is organic with his novels; both grow out of the same youth in Anatolia, the same upheavals, dreams, agonies, and hopes. He richly evokes the Kimindenia region in *Beyond the Aegean;* and he does the same in "On the Kimindenia," a narrative that could have been brought into the novel itself. The Aegean setting is constructively and poetically developed in "The Seagulls" and "No Passage." Andreas Karandonis remarks on the use of the Aegean: ". . . [I]t is not the familiar classical sea with the palpable, the material poetry of its watery reality. . . ." [2] Karandonis continues to describe Venezis' symbolic use of the Aegean as a means of self-realization, as a force for drawing out love, and as a trap or barrier which sharpens human loneliness. He deals with the Saroniko in the same way. In *Serenity*, the novel, he describes its barren mountains; in the short stories, "People of the Saroniko" and "Moment on the Saroniko," among others, he exploits the same setting. Themes and symbols reappear in the shorter fiction —the blind gods, the bitter fate to which man must be resigned, the exhausting struggle which, whether it conquers or fails, results in death, the only certainty.

After *Manolis Lekas,* whose title story has already been considered, Venezis published *The Aegean.* Its thirteen stories may be divided into two parts: those which deal with themes of this world and those which deal with the dream world. *The Aegean* definitely represents the author's creative powers at their height and is a product of his youth and early striving for recognition. Passion and craft join, and when the union succeeds the result is memorable art.

LIOS—Such is the case with "Lios," one of the first tales which Venezis wrote after his Turkish imprisonment ended in 1923.[3] It focuses on the "Bat," a young one-armed man named Petros. When the Bat was fifteen, he went with a detachment of Greeks to Gymnos, an island near Turkey. The Turks raided the island slaughtering all the Greeks but him. Wounded in the arm, he escaped by hiding in a cave. When he was found, his arm had rotted and was amputated.

His life is filled with Turkish and Greek violence. As a youth, he watched three Turks being put to death vengefully by Greeks. They were made to walk a plank into the sea. Only one of the Turks knew how to swim; and when he did not sink, the populace stoned him till the sea was red with blood. The Bat threw a stone himself and watched the helpless Turk sink.

To remember these bloody incidents he has had himself tattooed with a lion, snakes, a gorgon, and a bat, symbols of the savagery he has known. The tattooed bat gives Petros his nickname. As refugee Aivaliotes, he and his father are now fishermen on Lesbos. Their nets and hooks carried off by the sea, they must go into debt to buy new ones. The Bat's father consents to his fishing off the island of Lios, Turkish territory, to bring home a good catch that will help pay off the debt. If caught, the young man will be jailed and fined, and his boat and nets confiscated.

The Turkish soldier who captures the young Greek poacher has been aided in the chase by two Turkish fishermen from Crete. The soldier, the fishermen, and the Bat spend the night reminiscing. The soldier has been pressed into service reluctantly and wishes he were home. The fishermen are refugees from Crete, where they were prosperous, and miss their island. They persuade the soldier to release the boy. As the Bat leaves, the soldier shoots a seagull. Astounded, the Bat wonders at the kindness of the fishermen and the soldier; the soldier cannot understand why he must kill the gull.

When the Bat returns to Lesbos, he goes to the local tattoo artist to have him commemorate the incident. The artist wants to tattoo him with another gorgon, but the young man decides instead to have a seagull tattooed on his shattered arm. Despite the pain of the needle, Petros is happy as the gull takes shape.

Here, as in his novel, *Number 31328*, Venezis chronicles the effect of wartime savagery on people. The Bat is humanized by the kindness of the fishermen and the soldier. The seagull, symbol of life for the fishermen, themselves standing for gentleness and peace, marks the incident for the Bat. In slaying the gull, the Turkish soldier has purged his longing for the enemy's blood.

The chronologically organized story is interrupted to flash back on the two most significant incidents in the Bat's life, the massacre of the Greeks on Gymnos and the drowning of the Turks. How these events affect his character is shown by his reactions. Like Venezis' other characters, the Bat is simply drawn. He is incapable of analyzing his actions and responses. He can only perceive his confusion at his release by the Turkish soldier; he cannot really understand why he is confused. At critical moments, like that of his release, the Bat's puzzlement requires some active response, similar to the earlier responses but somehow different. For example, although he is tattooed again, as he had been after the massacre of the Greeks on Gymnos, his tattoo this time is a seagull and not a fearsome bat or gorgon.

The sentences are fairly short and the pace rapid. Venezis typically slows down in a descriptive passage when, as the omniscient author, he analyzes actions or character. In describing the dancing of the Greek guerrillas who are massacred at Gymnos, he writes:

When they danced to the austere beat of the drums, their movements, spare and ritualized, repeated the rhythm. . . . For these men of fiery blood, inflamed by the slightest affront, this characteristic of the dance was an unburdening of the heart, the same deep need that causes every man to lose his individuality in the conscience of the mass.[4]

The seagull as a beneficent symbol recurs in other stories. Venezis generally poses the gentle bird against some ravenous bird or animal—the bat here, the crow elsewhere. The sea setting evokes a tranquil tone of resignation and submission, for the sea, while it is part of the earth, is a special cosmos governed by its own laws and peopled by monsters and gorgons. To sail the sea, when it is a man's heritage, is a compulsion from which there is no escape. Like earth living, sea life is hard and grim. Seldom does man's struggle alter the scheme of things on earth or on the sea. In "Lios" it is the chance presence of kindness in the fishermen that affects the soldier and, in turn, the Bat. The soldier's humane act challenges and alters what both he and the Bat regard as a fixed course of events. While this story ends positively, in "Akif," the snake, destroyer of humanity, prevails.

AKIF—Akif is a Turkish rural guard in Lesbos. Strong and busy, he is pleased with himself, his pretty wife, and their small son, Mehmet. His face has the undisturbed look of a man who is at peace with himself and life because his demands have been fulfilled. Akif's composure is shattered when he encounters a huge snake. The monster slithers forth as Akif attempts to clear the opening from which issues the stream irrigating the orchards. The confrontation is shattering for the man: it destroys his manliness.

For a year and a half he will not leave his shack. His prosperity dwindles; his wife sells their olive trees, keeping only one small grove. A whirlwind passing through the village spares all but Akif's trees. Now, faced with complete poverty, Akif is powerless to work or take an interest in life. His final loss is the discovery of his neglected wife in the arms of another man. When Akif sends her away, he and the boy Mehmet are left alone. Akif's wife dies soon after and Akif himself falls ill. The Christians say he killed a sacred snake whose spirit pursues him. Akif, although unwilling to admit belief in this story, secretly suspects it might be true.

With Akif's illness, an ugly Christian woman comes to care for him and his son. She is iron-willed, fat, scarred, and even mustached. But Akif needs her care and asks her to stay. In time, she hangs on the wall on icon depicting Saint George slaying the dragon. Akif is dismayed at the sight of this huge snake and thinks he will be unable to endure having the picture in his shack. But she is adamant; he can post pictures of his own saints, she tells him. So, Akif becomes accustomed to the picture of the "snake." His life begins to settle and, again, he takes a job as the rural guard. Dominated by a shrewish wife, his life bleak, his son lost to him, he even comes to look upon the snakes he meets in a

friendly way. The wretchedness of his life is brought home to him
by the happiness of Ahmet, a neighboring peasant. Although
Ahmet and his wife and two children work hard, they are joyful
and thrive. Spitefully, Akif destroys the tobacco plants Ahmet and
his family grow in their garden.

During the population exchange of 1922, Akif boards the ship
going to Turkey.[5] But he is ordered to return to Lesbos, the only
Turk to be left behind. Being the rural guard, he must point out
the Turkish estates on the island to the Greeks. As Akif disem-
barks alone, two villagers exclaim that the snake which had attacked him many years ago has appeared in the same place. Akif
rushes wildly to find the snake. Enraged, he tries to clear the
plugged opening of the irrigation pipe with a stick. He must kill
the snake in order to confirm its reality. "Otherwise, there could
be no justification, no explanation for anything." [6] But the monster has vanished. Only some twigs are blocking the water from
running freely.

"Akif lies in the ditch, his hands fallen, his white head on the
mud, his eyes still. The barrenness is unendurable. As Akif lies
there, he sees a perpendicular line, a cypress, biting the sky" (p.
79).

Thus Venezis ends the story with the snake symbol which has
destroyed Akif's life.[7]

"Akif" begins with a description of how the olive groves stretch
from the mountains to the sea. "In the depths of the bay sleep the
ancient sea gods of the Aegean. Only once each eon, on moonless
nights, they waken and appear. They come to the beaches and ask
the trees that are almost as ancient as they, whether they have
heard in the forests anything about Pan and the Satyrs. The leaves
rustle lightly to answer, 'No, nothing.' 'Do they still live?' ask the
embittered seagods. And the olives, unshaken in their certainty,
reply, 'Oh, how can they have died!'" (p. 57). The rest of the
story sketches a cruel world in which Akif, strong, young, fearless,
becomes a coward through a chance encounter with a monstrous
snake. If Pan and the seagods are benign, then they are indeed
dead. This is a world in which events seem purposeless, governed
by chance. This is the world of the snake, terrifying and incomprehensible. Akif fails because he cannot sustain his courage in
the face of the horrible existence of the snake. The fact that the
villagers say it is a sacred snake and that Akif identifies it with the

dragon in the icon of Saint George suggests its status as a theological symbol. If it is a symbol of evil, or of the devil, Venezis implies that it strikes blindly. No moral order in which good is rewarded and evil punished is apparent in Akif's world. Akif, a good man, is struck down like Job. Not having Job's courage, patience, and accessibility to God, he succumbs without understanding why.

As a character, Akif, like Manolis Lekas, is remarkable. While Manolis remains a doer in spite of his victimization by fate, Akif becomes a passive victim after he encounters the snake early in the story. Manolis is admirable in that he wrestles with himself and his fate incessantly. In contrast, Akif arouses only pity for he epitomizes the defeated spirit. The opportunity to kill the snake definitely eludes him even at the end of the story. Manolis, although he is struck down, is one of Venezis' few tragic characters. He strives to change himself; he tries to change the lot of his youngest son.

Such characters risk everything, including themselves, in an attempt to alter things, things which seem fixed to the Akifs. When such characters lose, they are truly tragic; they portend hope, however, for they show man at his highest level of humanity. The victims who submit completely do not. Akif is a mere plaything, a piece of wood, a tenpin, in the game of life. Manolis, by his resistance, asserts his human reason and feeling. For Manolis Lekas, as for Petros, the Bat, in "Lios," better men in a better world are possible; for Akif, the most moving of Venezis' victims, death is the only existence on and in the earth. It is appropriate that Akif is a Muslim, for unquestioning submission to fate is a part of his creed. Indeed, the influence of the Muslim view of man and the world seems to have impressed Venezis. This is not surprising in view of his personal background and experience.

Although Akif, like Manolis Lekas, is static and one-dimensional, he is less a vague symbolic type than some of Venezis' other characters. In the later stories the Akifs are more shadowy and generalized, like the defeated general in "Theonichos and Mnisarete."

THE SEAGULLS—In "The Seagulls," Barba ["Uncle"] Dimitri, a lighthouse keeper on an island, has lost his two sons in the Anatolian catastrophe of 1922. Now an old man, he has withdrawn from

human society. He rarely visits the neighboring island to pray before the icon of the Virgin, something he had done as a younger
man. His only companions are two seagulls, which he has raised
and named for his dead sons. Flying off during the day, the gulls
return to spend the night at his hut. One night they fail to return.
When a young man and his girl swim across to the lighthouse
island, Barba Dimitri learns from them that some young men shot
the gulls for sport. Barba Dimitri's loneliness is immeasurable.
"His tears fall on the dry earth. Above him the beacon of the
lighthouse beams and fades regularly, on and off, austerely and
inevitably, like the dark powers of life, fate, and death." [8]

THE ROAR—In "The Roar," another story in *The Aegean,* a dying
old woman recalls a look she had received from Dimitri, long ago.
Now, she recognizes it as the glance of love because she has recently seen it on the faces of a boy and girl who come to pray at a
nearby shrine in a cove. The old woman had not married Dimitri
but a sailor, who was lost at sea. Her sons were seamen, too. Now,
she weeps for the love she never knew, "the music she never heard
because she blindly submitted to the fate of men—men who have
no rights." [9] I.M. Panayotopoulos remarks, "This old woman in
'The Roar' is a prototype and symbol found throughout the prose
works of Venezis. Most of his characters are simple, well-inten-
tioned, patient, submissive before the will of God and fate." [10]

THE BIRD—"The Bird" seems to be a biographical reminiscence
since the family involved somewhat resembles Venezis' family.
One of the dead sisters with whom the young man in the story
played and dreamed is Artemis. Venezis' own sister, Artemis, died
in 1918. The story concerns a bird which the mother brings from
the family's island home. The brother and sister feel sorry for the
caged bird and want to release it. When they finally do, the bird
refuses to fly away. The sister is stunned. "I would never have
believed it," she murmurs, truly alarmed. "So much then can one
get used to being caged!"
    "So much, my child," answers the white-haired mother.[11]

THE OTHER STORIES—In "No Passage" Venezis shows us two
women who try to escape their lives as prostitutes. Boarding a
small boat for Neapoli, three miles distant, they try to flee Myti-

lene. Jealously, they deface a photo forgotten on the boat by a young girl, whose photographed face represents everything that they are not. In the end, they must return to Mytilene despite their dreams and their urgent desire to escape their lot. For them there is no passage anywhere. Freedom is impossible. Their attempt is a gesture of futile protest.

Of the remaining stories "The Caique of the Theseion" is notable. Again demonstrating the bondage of men to fate, it deals with a man who becomes a builder to escape the sea. All the men in his family before him have been seamen, but he is determined to elude fate. He charts his life carefully, puts off marrying, and gains a reputation as a good builder. One day, he turns on a scaffolding at Tourkolimano to look at the sea and falls. Paralyzed from a bad break in his leg, he must give up building. He goes to Athens where he opens a kiosk overlooking the Temple of Theseus. Only once does he journey back to Tourkolimano. Although the sea has ruined his leg, he feels he has successfully escaped its clutches. In 1942, during the war, he tries to find a safe way to invest his savings and decides to buy wood. In order to prevent the German invaders from confiscating it, he builds a caique. At first he seeks a buyer for his boat, but finally it becomes a necessary part of his life. He watches over it daily. He calls the pigeons landing on it gulls; a white one stands for good and a black one for bad. Thus, despite his well-laid plans to flee the sea, it has trapped him.

The best story in the second part of the book, "Themes of the Dream World," is entitled "Tale of the Aegean." A boy born blind must move to the city with his mother. Because she must work as a stonebreaker, she leaves him alone. One day, he gets lost, and she is frantic. To keep him from being alone, she apprentices him to the local circus, where he is trained to handle snakes. His act is most successful. With the snakes entwined about his neck, he taps their mouths which they open. One night, as his mother sleeps embracing him, she feels his small fingers tapping her arm. She understands and weeps painfully.

" 'Why?' she asks God. 'In what did I err?' But the silence around her is deep and the darkness dense." [12]

In *The Aegean* the world Venezis sketches is ruthless. Good and evil forces seem to battle ceaselessly. Justice seldom operates, although, on occasion, excessive arrogance or boastful well-being is punished. More often, misfortune strikes without reason. If existence seems purposeless, Venezis, nevertheless, shows that some human happiness is possible. This is achieved through dynamic acceptance of the terms of life. The more human man becomes in contrast to the cruel inhuman cosmos, the more fully he lives and knows *yalini* or peace. He must fight to change his fate, but he risks total defeat like Akif if his strength falters. The alternative is to retreat and live a careful and restrained life. This more definitely results in failure and loss. The builder in "The Caique of the Theseion" is an example of one who has foregone living by giving up his sea heritage. Whereas the builder does not sense his loss fully, Stavros Valmas does in "The Final Hour." While men must submit and accept failure, there is merit in the heroic struggle. Peace, serenity, comes only with the submission that follows the struggle. To give up striving, to become passive, is to die. In *The Aegean* the struggle seems to involve some humane act performed against inhumanity or senseless monstrosity. To assert humanity in this perverse world is man's fate. To accept his condition brings peace.

Based on these philosophical premises, few of the stories have causal plots. More often, events occur because of the way of the world rather than because of probability and necessity. The incidents tend to illustrate the themes Venezis presents. Karandonis' discussion of the author's aims in *Serenity* could be applied to the short stories of *The Aegean*. Venezis ". . . cites, develops, and shows with his symbolic tales . . . his view of Life and Fate (Moira), concluding that the fate of man is death and that what is left us is to withstand with the chimerical hope, the lyrical dream, the creative act, moral perseverance, and the conscientious practice of an evangelical goodness." [13]

The characters are generally simple and unsophisticated, static rather than dynamic, one-dimensional rather than multidimensional, pathetic rather than tragic. They act instinctively and seldom can analyze their deeds and reactions. The omniscient point of view is hence used to definite advantage in that the author can explain what his characters cannot.

Venezis excels in the use of the demotic language. His dialogue is direct and colloquial. It abounds in colorful regional talk, quite often poetic. His descriptive passages sustain the spare and simple lyrical quality. In "The Roar" Venezis writes:

In East Samos the sea is never quiet. The sirocco begins early in the summer. Only at nightfall does the wind die, and then, in the deep seas, in the clear night light, one by one the distant Dodocanese islands are discerned: Kos and Kalymnos. They can be seen till the night is over; then they return again to the deep Aegean from which they came.[14]

The critic Karandonis writes about *The Aegean:* "These stories evoke a golden poetic tone, taking us down roads more easily traveled, in the familiar atmosphere of *Serenity* but in territory more Venezian . . . where the personal lyrical dream dominates utterly. . . . Narrative achievements like 'The Seagulls,' 'Lios,' 'The Bird,' 'The Roar' expose a craft that has reached its perfection."[15] Examples of this craft are amply evidenced also in *Winds*, the author's third collection of short stories.

II Winds

In these stories life is subject to the winds of chance.[16] Characters have little control over their fates; their choices and reactions are determined, more often than not, by the unpredictable nature of life rather than by the causality of events or characters. The stories show Venezis' "most organic quality . . . a sensitivity that vigorously reacts even to the slightest contact with the blind body of life."[17] *Winds* includes the long story "Theonichos and Mnisarete," which later appears in the collection *The Defeated.* It has also been translated into German.[18]

"On the Kimindenia," a realistic story, contrasts with "Theonichos and Mnisarete," in which romantic and realistic elements interplay. They both show Venezis at his best and indicate the scope of his versatility. "Mount of Olives" continues the story of Akif, one of Venezis' most unforgettable characters. The episode narrated in this story was used in *Above the Flames,* a radio play commemorating the fortieth anniversary of the Asia Minor catastrophe of 1922.[19] "The Final Hour" and "Mycenae" both illustrate characters who, through a new experience, come to have a deeper understanding of life and death. In "Death," the sensitive main character, confronted by the certainty of death, tries to grasp the fullness of life and misses.

ON THE KIMINDENIA—The main character is the overseer of the estate. His quick wit (he saves some oxen from drowning) and his bravery (he leads others to put out a fire) result in his being made overseer. Once he assumes this job, he is no longer the simple man he was as a peasant. He cannot sleep; he constantly frowns. He has dedicated his whole life to his master. Once he thought about marrying, but his sense of duty to his master curbs this desire.

The story then reveals the overseer through his actions in relation to Sari, the sick ox, and Paraskeva, the sick Lemniote. In spite of the ploughman's protestations that the ox is dying, the overseer insists on yoking the ox. At the same time he announces, in the hearing of the dying Paraskeva, his workman, that shirking and sickness will not be tolerated. Those who are sick, he says, must go. Paraskeva, like other men from Lemnos, comes to work at harvest time then embarks again for Lemnos in the winter. But this winter he has been unable to return home. He has lain deathly ill.

The overseer orders the ox Sari to be hitched up to Christos' plough. Christos, who is lighthearted and sings while he works, becomes sober and melancholy. He does not whip the ox; he watches it sway and stumble as it pulls. He wipes clean the open sore on its back. When the ploughmen break for lunch, they burst out against the overseer's cruelty. "Nor God, nor Turk can stomach this," comments the Pergamiote. Another says, "Why involve God? Didn't you see how the overseer dismissed the Lemniote whose days are ending? Do you expect the overseer to feel more for an ox?" [20] They agree that Paraskeva isn't worth any more than an ox to the overseer. A great silence overcomes them as they reflect how little is their worth as men. Christos indignantly decides to take the sick ox back to the estate. The overseer tries to stop him and they fight. When the overseer sees the hostility of the other ploughmen, he withdraws vengefully.

The next night, the Lemniote dies beset by dreams of all the overseers he had ever worked for. He is unable to say what message he wants sent to his wife. When the overseer, who has been sleepless because of a bad conscience as well as an injury to his pride, is awakened, he comes to see Paraskeva's corpse. From Paraskeva's pillow rolls out a wad of brightly colored calico he had saved as a gift for his wife when he went home. On Paraskeva's beard the overseer sees a fresh tear. Nauseated, he falls into his bed with a fever. At night, when he is better, he goes to see Sari the ox. He rubs some ointment into the ox's sore back.

"Poor Sari," he says. "What can I do for you? I don't have a heart" (p. 126). And he tenderly strokes the animal. The next day, Sari's carcass is thrown into the River of the Jackals. That night, the overseer dictates a letter which the Aivaliote writes:

"Your husband had back luck. He was sick for months. We buried him near the estate under a pine. I, the overseer, who am writing, will see that his *kantili* (a votive light) will burn all year for him. We are all sinners. I greet you" (p. 126).

Like "Manolis Lekas" this was written in 1927 when Venezis excelled in depicting events in the realistic style. As in *Number 31328* and "Manolis Lekas" the sentences are short and stripped bare of embellishments. The dialogue truly captures the simple, colloquial, and often figurative talk of the peasants. The spare quality, characteristic of Venezis' early prose works, appropriately reflects the grim lives and inarticulate characters of the peasants. The language, the tone, the characters, and the theme exhibit a Tolstoyan influence. The peasant overseer who dominates and acts like the master loses touch with the soil, animals, and men. He responds to Paraskeva's death with a guilt which racks him with fever. Reawakened, his humanity results in kindness and, as is illustrated in the letter to Paraskeva's widow, a simple religious humility. The winds of chance might account for the unrelenting nature of the world; but, although the chance death of Paraskeva bestirs the overseer's submerged humanity, his change is not due to chance but to his own choice. He has tried heartlessness and has been felled by it; sympathy for living things is better. It makes the grimness of life more tolerable. This favorite theme of compassion is reasserted and developed in many of the short stories and novels. The overseer, despite his errors, is a man who lives and struggles with life, unlike Stavros Valmas who is a living dead man.

THE FINAL HOUR—Stavros Valmas' life has been the walk from the office to his lodging. He has never changed jobs, married, loved, nor suffered, for risks are involved. Now, when death is upon him, he goes back to his birthplace, Anaplion, and climbs up to Palamidi. There, he meets the guide who shows him the fortress and its cells, the place where stood the guillotine, and the spot where rolled the severed heads. The guide also shows him the cell in which he had been imprisoned for murder for twenty years.

Stunned, Stavros asks why he had committed the murder. "For a woman," the guide answers.[21] The wife of a friend had been violated by the village bully, and since her husband was far away, the guide took it upon himself to exact justice. For the murder of the bully he was imprisoned. Later, when Palamidi was abandoned as a prison, he was freed because he had been a good prisoner. But he could not leave. He could no longer go down to live among men. Stavros asks him what became of the woman and her husband, the friend for whom he had murdered.

"I heard he died abroad," the guide answers, "and she remarried" (p. 19).

Stavros, upon hearing the story, has suddenly realized that his own life had been spent like the life of the guide.

"Why?" he asks. "Why did you wreck your life?"

The guide, serene and unmoved, replies, "I would do the same thing now, today" (p. 20).

Stavros is flooded with fear because he knows that, although the guide had been imprisoned, he had lived dynamically; Stavros, although he was free, had never lived.

The gods may be dead, but man's life has meaning only in proportion to the nobility with which he lives it. Akif, in *The Aegean,* is ruined because fear of the terrible snake haunts him; Stavros in "Final Hour" is neither free nor a man because he has not dared to act and suffer.

Another contrast with Stavros is the hermit in "Byzantium, Tokyo, and Andros." In the lonely Byzantine monastery on Andros, at the summit of a mountain, the hermit has the serenity that comes with noble commitment, responsibility, and suffering. He lovingly tends the Byzantine relics, some of which turn to dust when touched. No other monk will stay at the isolated monastery; he tends it alone. Like the seaman, who was prisoner of the Japanese in Tokyo and bore up bravely, so the hermit dedicated to preserving the religious heritage of Byzantium in Andros endures bravely. When a young girl visiting the monastery asks the old and sick hermit if he would make the same choice had he a second chance, he turns and answers her serenely.

"I have been happy. All is love. I came to the church with love." [22]

For Venezis, then, although the world is bereft of order and of God, men can find peace. They find it through exercising their limited freedom, whatever freedom can exist in a world governed by fickle chance. They must choose, and they must stand by their choice with deep conviction. They must love deeply and suffer greatly. Like the ancient Greek heroes, they must be epic in their emotional responses and struggles. Only then do they live; only then are they genuine men.

DEATH—In *"Death"* (1927), an early and powerfully realistic story included in *Winds,* the hunchback peasant Gregory knows he must die when his spine slips to a spot that he has marked with a button on his garments. Working hard in spite of this knowledge, he weathers the village scoffers. Hopelessness overcomes him when he is cheated by the master of his rightful share of money for his work in the fields. Venezis contrasts the bleakness of his life and the terrible knowledge and final desire for death with a short, lyrical, descriptive passage affirming life: ". . . Beyond, on the gulf, the sea trembles in a golden light. The time has come for the swallows to leave. There falls with the autumnal night winds a fresh dew savoring of the salty sea. A bird perching on the rose-bush in the yard chirps happily.

"It might have been a sparrow." [23]

Although death must be, death implies the continuity of life.

THEONICHOS AND MNISARETE—The notion that death as well as love is ever present is heavily underscored in "Theonichos and Mnisarete." This story combines both mythic and gothic elements. The setting, site of the Kerameikon archaeological excavations, exploits the ancient heritage. Never in Greece can man escape his mythological past, the dead past. For the elderly watchman, who lives with his wife in a hut on the grounds, the Kerameikon (site of an ancient monastery) is a tranquil resting place for friends. Daily, he inspects the graves and monuments, chatting about the occupants to his wife as if they were alive. She, on the other hand, regards her life as desperate and ugly. She detests their residence among the dead and questions her husband daily for news about their living neighbors. The old man tells her that a man has come to live in the ruined red tower overlooking the cemetery. The new occupant, a defeated general, shutters the windows overlooking the street where living people pass and looks out only at the dead. The bizarre and racked red tower, the living-dead vanquished general, who once commanded grand armies, the stormy spring, the ghostly howling, the gravesite setting—these comprise some of the gothic elements of the story.

In the springtime, the archaeologists come to excavate, and the old man has much to tell his wife about the newfound graves. The most notable discovery is the ancient skeletons of two young lovers, Theonichos and Mnisarete. The skeletons cannot be dislodged from the earth for they will crumble to pieces. Because it will rain, the old watchman wants the archaeologist to cover the skeletons with some earth. But it cannot be done; the skeletons must remain as they are, forever in an uncovered grave, winter and summer. The old man is terrified and begins his homeward trip during the thunderstorm. On the way he hears the voices of some young lovers and recognizes them in a flash of lightning to be the same youths who were there before. He insists on their leaving and goes home beset by fear. In trying to calm him, his wife seeks an explanation of his terror. The old watchman tells her that the preservation of the skeletons through thousand of years is sacred and miraculous. Theonichos and Mnisarete had faith that in their graves the living could no longer hurt them. Now, the old man feels, something barbarous and inhuman has happened in the violation of their graves. As he tries to explain his feelings to his wife, the storm breaks. Through the frightening thunder and lightning the old couple cling to one another and pray. When the wind and rain blow through the open window into the house, the old woman beseeches her husband to seal the grave. In a panic he goes into the darkness and rain, and while she tremblingly waits, she hears a howling like that of a wounded man during the noises of the storm. When her husband returns, his leg is broken for he has fallen into an excavation on his way to strew earth over the graves of Theonichos and Mnisarette. In the hole the old man had also heard the terrible howling which came, he thinks, from the ruined red tower. Now, again, the two old people hear a moaning which rises to a shriek as they cower and pray.

When fall comes, the old man's wife is dead, and he has aged since the accursed night. He hears the moaning and shrieking nightly and recalls with terror that rainy spring night. One day, the young lovers who were in the cemetery that same stormy night return. The old watchman tells them the story of this "climactic night, perhaps the last great night of his life, the night that has racked him. It is necessary that he live and relive it, as necessary as light and sleep. The end of the journey nears, and memory must be strong, so that life may not seem wasted, so that it can be justified." [24]

When the young people go to look at the graves of Theonichos and Mnisarete, a storm breaks. They take refuge in a domelike vault and there consummate their love. With the end of the storm, they knock at the watchman's door and ask him to unlock the gate so they may leave. The old man is frightened that they should have been out among the graves in the darkness. But that night when the old man listens for the moaning and shrieking sounds, they do not come. They never come again, "for Theonichos and Mnisarete have again found tranquillity; again they rest peacefully in the earth" (p. 50). The curse of the ancients disturbed in their graves is lifted because the young lovers have found happiness nearby.

Like Venezis' other stories "Theonichos and Mnisarete" has a loosely constructed plot. The lovers, for example, do not come to the Kerameikon out of the necessity of events. Their reappearance is not made probable in terms of plot. They appear because chance dominates the world of Venezis. Vague and shadowy as characters, they are obvious symbols, living extensions of the dead lovers. They must be allowed to consummate their love to mitigate the desecration of the graves of the dead ancients. In Greek mythology the unburied dead were restless since they could never make the journey to the underworld. Here, it is only through another love that the disturbed dead can rest.

The defeated general is an even vaguer character. Another symbol, he stands for all those whom life has broken senselessly. The old guard and his wife are very generally sketched. The absurd world emerges as Venezis' strongest character. Its unchanging nature from the ancient past to the present is underscored. Man becomes a shadow in his battle against this violent and incomprehensible cosmos. Perhaps, this is why Venezis' characters are so symbolic and vague. Yet, the power of this story might have been increased had we learned more about the defeated general, the lovers, and the old guard. Venezis' early stories, while including nostalgic and delicately lyrical passages as well as outright romantic elements, never lose touch with reality. In "Theonichos and Mnisarete" the reader moves among symbols, not characters, in a fanciful and dead world. Symbols cannot elicit pity or terror, joy or laughter. Like that of Antaeus, Venezis' strength seems to ebb as he loses touch with the soil of the countryside and his youth. I. M. Panayotopoulos observes that when Venezis foregoes autobiographical experiences, he "gets farther from himself and from the area in which he is truly competent." [25]

MYCENAE—In "Mycenae" the reader is again shown how the ancient world influences the modern one. The aim of Katherine Ralli, an Anatolian Greek widow, is to rear her son to be a man in the genuine sense of the word. She tells him stories of far-off places, buffeted by strong winds and fierce storms. He learns of the men of the sea, "who all their lives fight the sea, the cold, and the spirits of the sky. They worship the lightning bolt that writes fire in the darkness; they have hard hands, and their hearts are beaten by violent winds as are their bodies. But in the hour of crisis their hearts prove pure and spotless because they have done their duty to life: to fight and to suffer much." [26]

When Philip is old enough, Katherine tells him about Greece. The ancient gods are

. . . beings like men who play with joy, hunt in the forests, love, and struggle. They were neither austere nor ascetic; they were omnipotent, governing the winds, fire, and lightning. But they lacked the grandeur of men, the grandeur of death. They were immortal. They never knew in that secret hour the horror, the message of the other world, that gives men the right to be weak, great and alone: the terror of death (p. 52).

Under such gods lived Greece's ancient heroes. Katherine recounts the myth of Agamemnon. The boy listens and tries to recapture " the spirit of sacrifice, the motive of heroic actions, the strength of serenity" (p. 53).

When Philip grows older, Katherine and he visit Mycenae one spring. The young shepherd of whom they ask directions knows only that this place is where his grandfather Kakavas' sheep graze. But an old shepherd, who looks like an ancient king, shows them the way. He looks directly at them, unlike the Anatolian shepherds who know fear at the hands of the Turk and cannot look men directly in the eyes. He is Greece, Katherine thinks.

Philip and Katherine visit Agamemnon's tomb. She cannot

enter Clytemnestra's tomb because there was nothing heroic, she feels, about Clytemnestra's actions. What can she say to her son about Clytemnestra? How can she tell him of that horror? The boy plucks a yellow flower at the Lion's Gate and brings it into Agamemnon's tomb to lessen the great hero's loneliness.

Katherine returns to Mycenae many years later, alone, a grieving mother. Her son has been lost in the Anatolian catastrophe. She revisits Agamemnon's tomb and remembers her son's wonder. She decides to enter Clytemnestra's tomb. Suddenly, she sees Agamemnon from another point of view. Greedy for the gold and the slave girls of Troy, he did not hesitate to sacrifice Iphigenia. Clytemnestra's vengeance on Agamemnon and Cassandra was exacted for her daughter. When Katherine leaves the tomb, she finds a yellow flower growing in the barren soil. Plucking it, she lays it on Clytemnestra's tomb, so that a mother, the mother of Iphigenia, will not be lonely.

The world of Venezis here demands that man act nobly and heroically. Katherine rears her son by this dictum. But what is heroism, what is nobility? Katherine sees that heroic actions look different when seen from the victim's point of view. She learns the difference between Homer and Euripides. Like one of the Trojan women she is victimized by a war out of which heroic poetry can be made. She has looked only at the ideal; now she knows the real. Yet, the spirit of the ancients, the idealized heroic spirit, has been necessary to sustain the life of Greece. Venezis contrasts the proud bearing of the free Greek with the servility learned under the Turk by the Anatolian Greek.

THE OTHER STORIES—In the world of Venezis the gods are dead or heedless, although their phantoms haunt the Greeks. The Anatolian catastrophe—a senseless event—occurs, and Philip is killed. In "Mount of Olives" Akif observes Ramadan twice and the villagers justify his forgetfulness. "His God has forgotten him; why should he not forget?" [27] And on the night of Holy Easter, Akif and Vasilis, the Christian, as they review their agonized lives, ask the same question, "In what did we err?" (p. 95). Akif kneels to pray with the Christian, and Venezis observes that they pray to "two distant Gods whose faces are turned from men" (pp. 95–6).

In "Anastasimo," (Easter Hymn) the two women, the betrothed and the mother, grieve for the man who will never return from the Turkish labor battalions.[28] For Akif and them there can never be an Easter. If the Redeemer lives, He has forgotten their existence.

The same theme is underscored in "Moment on the Saroniko" in which a young woman searches for the perfect place to consummate her love. The sacredness of her action and the immortality of the moment are tainted by the meaningless death of a swimmer. "Another day destroyed," observes the girl bitterly.[29] ". . . She is certain that the irreparable is done. That day, too, must continue the story of mankind, the bitter story of mankind" (p. 68). The beautiful moment, the deathless moment, must be killed by the terrifying consciousness of death, the only certainty.

These and other stories in *Winds* show Venezis moving from the powerful realism of the 'twenties and 'thirties to the only occasionally successful romanticism of the 'forties. Yet these stories demonstrate more consistently the craftsmanship evident in *The Aegean* than do those of the two later collections. Venezis masterfully describes the desolate landscape in which his embattled peasants move. Many of the characters, like the overseer in "On the Kimindenia" and Gregory the hunchback in "Death," spring to life movingly and truthfully. The later stories begin to show characters who exist as obvious types for didactic purposes. The themes, however, are still those of *The Aegean:* man must struggle to assert his humanity in an inhuman world which God and the gods have forgotten.

Venezis' evocative style "is related to silence, to the unspoken word, to the stillness and elusive music of spare expression, rather than to outright sound, to the movement and color of polished and plastic prose style." [30] His language suggests rather than explains, evokes rather than states. It is, at its best, the Chekhovian language of understatement in which a magical aura is created by what is left unsaid.

His two best collections of short stories appeared during the war, at the height of his country's agony. Some of his later stories, such as those in *Wartime,* continue to reflect Venezis' profound concern with the tragedy of the Greek people. However, it is in his play, *Block C,* and in his novel of the Occupation, *Exodus,* that one finds his major response to the great and sad drama of war.

CHAPTER 4

The Drama of War

I *Introduction*

ELIAS Venezis did not serve in uniform during the Second World War. Throughout the defeat and Occupation he worked in Athens for the Bank of Greece. Each day he could eat at his favorite restaurant (when food was available) and sleep at night, if he wished, in his own bed. He wrote constantly. And yet, as fate would have it, he was imprisoned by the Gestapo, sentenced to death, and escaped a firing squad only because of public protest raised in his behalf. The most immediate and concrete literary result of the trauma was *Block C,* the author's one full-length play.[1] It is a grim drama that had a mixed reaction when first performed by the National Theater on December 5, 1945. Since then the play has been given regularly throughout the provinces of Greece and on Cyprus.[2] Although Venezis has written no other long plays, he has contributed to contemporary drama in another capacity: after retiring from the Bank of Greece in 1957, he became advisory director of the Greek National Theater.

Venezis, of course, does not need the genre of the play in order to dramatize the effects of war. He has the short story and the novel. Many of the stories in his five collections deal with the wartime problems of the Greek people. According to Hatzinis, the tensions of war brought out the best in the genius of both Myrivilis and Venezis. It is in the novel *Exodus* that the latter makes his fullest response to this second epochal defeat. This upheaval differs drastically from the Catastrophe of 1922; then, a generation earlier, the defeat offered no chance for regrouping, for resistance, for eventual victory. The expulsion of the Greeks from Anatolia was complete and irrevocable; the Great Powers, with whom Greece had been allied a few years before, now ranged themselves solidly on Turkey's side. In the second catastrophe, the defeat and Occupation of 1941, there was struggle, both political and military; there was resistance and eventual triumph. And the

Western Allies (England and the United States) ranged themselves solidly against only one aspect of Greece: the political Left.

Yet before the victory, as Venezis himself states, the German
enemy practiced a mechanistic barbarism many times worse than
the human barbarism of the Turks under whom he had suffered in
the labor battalions. His writings on the Occupation, therefore,
are often charged, like *Block C*, with a deeper moral fervor, a
clearer patriotic purpose, a purer tragic sense.

Exodus, published in 1950, has the sub-title, "The Book of the
Occupation." It is that, but only in a restricted manner; a hundred
novels may be given such a sub-title, and they still would record
only in part the bitterly fought years of enforced hospitality for
the "blond assassins" from the north. *Exodus* attempts to reflect
neither the political nor the military aspects of the Occupation; on
the contrary, it narrows itself to a kind of domestic tale about a
group of refugees who are incapable of meaningful struggle. They
are victims of their times, of their destiny; and the supposed sanctuary they seek, Athens, has nothing to offer them except famine
and death. That most of them are strangers brought together by
chance provides Venezis with a variety of cast and episode. That
they must move ahead through an ever-changing hostile environment presents the reader with suspense and horror as well as
courage, understanding, and pity. That the setting is Greece, the
land of classical tragedy, evokes both the mythical and the historical past in order to highlight the dramatic present.

Venezis' first major reaction in literature to the war is the play
Block C. Its subject matter stems directly from his own unforgettable peril. He stated the circumstances of his imprisonment in an
interview with L. Koukoulas published in the *Free Press* (June 2,
1945).[3] Another account of the event appears in the *Chronicle of
the Bank of Greece*.[4] The purpose of the interview with Koukoulas was to explore Greek thought in relation to the drama of the
Occupation, in this case *Block C*. The article provides us with the
very interesting background of the play.

At noon on October 28, 1943, a large crowd gathered in the big
hall of the Bank of Greece, in Athens, to honor the memory of
those who had fought the Italian fascists in Albania, and to express their faith in freedom. The meeting was illegal. Just as a
veteran of the Albanian campaign was speaking, the S.S. men arrived. They fired their automatics at the crowd of fifteen hundred

people. Several were hit. Many hours of interrogation followed at the end of which Elias Venezis and three others were called for by name and placed before a column of soldiers. As the Germans themselves said later, they had planned to execute the four right there; but the Director of the Bank intervened, saying that he had given permission for the meeting to be held. Since the Bank was involved, the Germans decided to go into the matter more deeply. As a result the four prisoners were taken to Merlin Street, to Gestapo headquarters. They were put into a room with a blinding light used for questioning. There they had to lie on the floor, a tall S.S. man standing over them. An officer came and stepped on their heads to keep them down. Venezis expected the officer to empty his gun into them. At dawn he and the others were hustled off to Averoff Prison.

The four were separated from the rest of the group that was going there; from something said by the S.S. officer to the director of the jail, Venezis knew their destination was to be "Block C." Each person was placed in a separate cell. Many condemned Greek patriots, now executed, had passed through "Block C." They had scratched their names on the walls with their fingernails in a last attempt to keep alive the remembrance of their sacrifice. For eighteen days and nights Venezis remained there, and every morning he expected to be taken out and shot. In the meantime the public protest against his detention and probable execution had grown to a significant magnitude; petitions and letters poured in to the German authorities not only from the Archbishop of Athens, Damaskinos, but also from many scientists, engineers, and intellectuals. The protest was so effective, Venezis states in the interview, that it must have reached Berlin. In any case, he was suddenly released. "When I was freed and learned what had happened in my behalf, I said that such a debt to humanity I could never repay in all my life." [5]

During the conversation Venezis expresses his belief that the Greek people ennobled themselves in their Resistance—with their passion for freedom, with their willingness to die for their country. He associates the Resistance "with the best hours" of Greek history. As for the future, Venezis declares his desire for a national climate that will allow the artists—poets, writers, and sculptors— to turn these noble events into myths and legends. On the subject of German cruelty, of their torture of innocents, Venezis recalls that he had known a barbarian rule once before, in Anatolia; but, he goes on, "Well, the fiercest Asiatic was an angel compared to the least soldier of the S.S." [6] Despite all that happened, Venezis does not hate the entire German people because not all were responsible for Nazism. Finally, in the interview, he refuses to speculate on what might have occurred to the Greek spirit had the Occupation lasted much longer. In his drama *Block C* he presents this spirit in perhaps its purest form—with the people as the tragic hero. Through struggle and sacrifice, through the gift of life they gave, they received eventually the gift of freedom.

II   *Plot and Structure of* Block C

The time and setting of the action, as indicated in the stage directions, are the summer of 1944 and Athens, when the Germans "fought with frightful terror to drown the popular resistance." [7] All the action occurs in that section of Averoff Prison to which the Germans had given the name "Block C." Seven condemned prisoners are held in a square cell; it is their fate, suspenseful and ominous, that commands the emotions of the audience. They include various types that allow for differentiation of response, attitude, and philosophy within the common circumstances: victims of capture, they are pawns in the grip of an implacable foe, a machine of terror and conquest. An act of sabotage —the blowing up of a bridge—has been committed. As a result the Germans have taken hostages—the seven who are now lodged in "Block C." They face almost certain death.

The prisoners include a sub-squadron commander in civilian dress, a partisan (one of the legendary *andartes*), a student, a diplomat, a citizen, an orderly, and a *saltadoros*. The last term grew out of the Resistance. Literally it means "leap-giver" and refers to one of the most dangerous acts in the struggle for freedom, leaping upon moving Nazi trucks and vans and often hijacking them in order to get food and other supplies for ELAS, the underground army. The deed became a specialty of daring young *saltadoroi* of EPON, the United All-Greece Youth Organization. In this activity many lost their lives.

The play opens in the semi-darkness of dawn with five forms lying asleep on straw mattresses in the cell. The first to stir is the partisan, who goes softly to the opening, the "eye" of the door, to listen outside. When the student gets up they discuss the thumping sounds they have heard all night—a call for help from some tortured victim of the Gestapo. Soon the three other prisoners are awake, the *saltadoros*, the diplomat, and the orderly. They talk about the dreaded Cell 71 from which no prisoner ever returns; and they wonder where the guards have taken one of their comrades, the sub-squadron commander. Will he be shot that morning? Has he cracked under torture? All the prisoners are gravely concerned except the orderly.

It is clear that he is not a patriot like the others. Between him and the *saltadoros*, the partisan, and the student the open animosity becomes increasingly bitter. When told about a comrade in Cell 71, the orderly cries, "And what can we do for him? Why did you wake me?" (p. 33). Soon after, they hear shots indicating that one or more hostages have been killed. The orderly suddenly tells the others that now they must take orders from him. "After the Germans, I command here" (p. 36). He curses when advised to read the executed man's name on the wall. The student calls him a worm after the orderly has said, "You moron, the only world for me is my own self" (p. 38). He beats his fist on his chest. Behind the name-calling and the hatred is the suspicion that the orderly is a spy for the Germans providing them with information gathered in the cell. The *saltadoros* tells the partisan quietly, "The other morning the orderly was absent outside. They took him to the S.S. for interrogation. They brought him back close to noon. And shortly afterward they came and took the sub-squadron commander" (p. 54).

In a plot whose main interest is the inevitable doom of the characters, where they are more acted upon than acting, every detail becomes charged with meaning. Sounds reaching the cell, such as boot thumps, chain rattles, and gunfire, can be signs of approaching peril. The opening of the cell door is particularly ominous, for it leads only to the enemy. The drama is a Sartrean *No Exit* where the disruption of the simplest ritual takes on significance. When the diplomat forgets to put on his necktie, it means that something is happening to his spirit. His friends understand because the same thing is happening to them.

Early in the morning, the Germans bring another hostage, the citizen Phaethon; he is dazed and incoherent. The *saltadoros* introduces him to the others. He lights a candle for the one dead and tells Phaethon he is to take the dead man's place. As he gradually comes to himself, Phaethon learns more and more about the cell and what to expect. Once in the morning and again in the afternoon they go out to the corridor for water. The educating of the new prisoner is tantamount to further exposition for the audience.

Inside the cell the strongest bonds develop among the activist types, the *saltadoros,* the partisan, and the student. The *saltadoros,* for example, privately explains to the partisan how the absent sub-squadron commander revealed self-incriminating details about his activities while he was delirious with fever. In turn the partisan warns the student to beware the orderly. He also tries to prepare the student, who is only nineteen, for the very worst. They have no right, he says, to regard death as ugly. More than death, however, the student fears torture.

Two dramatic actions conclude the first act: the abrupt removal of the student and the unexpected return to the cell of the sub-squadron commander, Pavlos Desilla. When the citizen Phaethon naively asks what will become of the student, the diplomat suggests that not to know one's fate is also torture. The only sure thing, he says, is the removal to Cell 71. "It is the cell of death" (p. 63). The sudden return, alive, of Commander Desilla greatly excites his comrade, the *saltadoros.* When he asks if anyone now there knows him, the *saltadoros* replies that only he and the orderly remain of the original group; the rest are new.

The long second act begins with a brief scene in the prison yard. It is afternoon of the same day, and the prisoners are outside for exercise. Through the barred window of the infirmary they hear talk about the sick and injured, and also about an act of sabotage the night before: the blowing up of a large bridge near Athens. From one of the windows comes a Greek song; then a Greek Red Cross girl enters the yard, and as each prisoner walks past her she whispers, "Courage." The sad and defiant song continues.

The rest of Act Two takes place in the cell. The partisan is very anxious about his young comrade, the student, who has not returned. In the dialogue Commander Desilla learns, mainly from the *saltadoros,* about the others. He assumes a protective attitude, typifying the ideal Greek Resistance hero. The orderly angrily wants them to quit talking nonsense when they discuss their feelings and their fate; he wants them to talk, instead, about the destroyed bridge. He mentions "bolsheviks." They hear sounds from outside; a German guard enters the cell and asks for the orderly. The two leave.

When they are alone, the prisoners speak more freely about themselves and their lives. Commander Desilla does not worry about himself, but about those still free who might yet be captured. In a few minutes the orderly returns and clashes with his fellow prisoners over a trivial matter. "What dog has moved my cards?" he cries (p. 88). Later, when questioned, he says he expects to go to Gestapo headquarters on Merlin Street. The Greek cook who brings their food secretly mentions the rumor that some of those to be executed for the sabotage of the bridge will be from the prison. He also brings in baskets of goods sent by their families; in the student's basket is a white flower from his sweetheart. They wonder if he is being tortured. Will he break?

While eating, the prisoners reminisce about their respective families. They eat bread and cheese which, along with roast lamb, is the symbolic fare of Greek patriots and *klephts* who fight in the mountains. They talk about the Lord's Supper; theirs, too, could be the last. At dawn they might die. They speak about the mythical gorgon (a favorite myth of Venezis) who searches the Aegean eternally for her lost brother, Alexander the Great. Commander Desilla tells the *saltadoros* that the gorgon lives in each of them, in their blood.

The student, Photis, is brought back with his arms slashed and salt poured on the open wounds. When he revives, his friends give him the basket and the white flower. Six hours he resisted, he says, and he kept to the same words, "I know nothing" (p. 120). That same night, however, they might take him to Gestapo headquarters. The investigation for the sabotage would begin that evening; and he fears that the Germans will rip off his fingernails. Soon the guards enter the cell again but not for the student; they take the meek citizen, Phaethon Philipakis. Once they leave, the partisan urges the student to name only him, the partisan, if he cracks under torture. "Although with our heart we say something else, our body may not hold out" (p. 125).

As the partisan suggests, they ask the guard if the student can see a doctor, but he cannot; it is forbidden. The diplomat, who has not said much during the second act, reads a poem written on the cell wall.

Here our life stands still
in the uncertain twilight
of our distant hopes.
All that we love
remains outside the door;
we left it there
when we passed the threshold.
                                        (p. 129)

Moments after the diplomat reads, a clamor of booted footsteps
sounds outside. The prisoners rise and gaze with agonized eyes at
the iron door. The guards grab the student again; a soldier hits
him with the butt of his gun. His comrades are stunned and solemn. The *saltadoros* picks up the white flower. "The young one,"
he says, "may not—may not return again" (p. 133).

The third and final act opens in the semi-darkness of dawn the
next morning. Neither the student nor the orderly has returned.
Soon they hear a commotion outside: the Germans are taking the
student to Cell 71, the death cell. The partisan cries, "He did not
bend! He did not inform! He remained true to Greece and to his
faith" (p. 139). A guard enters to retrieve the student's effects.
Commander Desilla wants Phaethon to get a note out of the
prison and take it to a certain address. Phaethon is afraid and
refuses; he has no stomach for heroic deeds.

The orderly, called a Judas by the *saltadoros*, returns to the cell
unharmed. The patriots question him about the student; they
taunt him and finally threaten him, and Commander Desilla
makes him admit that he told the Gestapo how he, Desilla, had
stolen from the German naval station certain documents about
embarkation. But the orderly insists he had no names to give the
Germans. Commander Desilla says, "Glory be to God. I alone will
pay" (p. 150).

Entering, a German officer begins to read off the names of the
condemned. Desilla demands a military court-martial as a prisoner of war, but he is told that it is too late; he is a hostage. The
interpreter tells them that at exactly six-thirty that morning they
will be executed. In a final speech Commander Desilla speaks to
his comrades, including the orderly who, ironically, will also be
killed, about a free Greece. "Do not make death ugly," he admon-
ishes (p. 155). The citizen Phaethon promises at last to do the
errand he had earlier refused to do. Desilla gives the *saltadoros*

his lucky charm. To the craven orderly he says, "Learn to be a man" (p. 157).

The *saltadoros* is left alone on stage. He sits and looks intently at the white flower. He puts fresh water in the can that holds the flower. Lighting a candle, he prays to God that He might help his condemned comrades. He hears the volley of shots. The *saltadoros* takes out a pencil, wets it with his lips, and starts writing the names on the wall. The opening of the door interrupts him; a new prisoner, half dazed, is pushed in. The *saltadoros* mutters, "Just or unjust." Falling to the floor, he embraces the feet of the stranger.

III   *Play and Performance*

Venezis dedicated *Block C* to the three friends with whom he actually spent "difficult days" in Averoff Prison. They are Criton Eleftheriades, Michael Pouskouris, and Elias Anastasiades. The chief virtue of the play, in fact, is not its aesthetic quality but its historical realism. Venezis footnotes the poem read by the diplomat as follows: "The verse of the poet Sub-Squadron Commander Michael Achilla, written in the jail. The Germans executed him at dawn on 5 June 1942" (p. 129). The cruel moment that *Block C* chronicles was very real, not only for the Greeks but for every nationality that suffered similar barbarism during the war. It is a kind of Passion Play for patriots, with the killing done through modern science, rather than primitive crucifixion. The author depends for effect on the audience's ability to empathize with the agony of its own heroes. He takes the aesthetic risk of assuming this emotional empathy. He also assumes his audience's knowledge of the character types in the cast; hence the characterization is less developed than the theme: the feelings and thoughts of doomed heroes facing death. The key question leading to a fuller realization of dramatic possibility is asked, "What have we done with our lives?" But the question is not pursued to the point where we truly know the characters.

If *Block C* is not a great play, it is nevertheless a good and interesting one; and its dramatic success is assured wherever an audience can be moved by man's inhumanity to man. That the play was not a smashing success when first performed by the National Theater may well reflect negatively on the sad times, the audience, and the theater itself. A full year of extremely bitter turmoil, since the Battle of Athens with its "December events" of

1944, had critically divided the Greek nation. A hot civil war between Right and Left, with British troops supporting the Right,
had created dark hatreds and turnabout loyalties. Liberation, the
dream of the condemned in *Block C*, was marred by class struggle
and Cold War; and those who were "glorious patriots" during the
Occupation (members of Resistance forces like EAM, the National Liberation Front, and its army ELAS) now became, as
Winston Churchill called them, "gangsters" and "criminals" dominated by the KKE, the Greek Communist Party.[8] At least four
characters in *Block C* would be identified as such by a sizeable
part of an Athenian audience in December, 1945. They are the air
force sub-commander, Pavlos Desilla; the partisan, Vassili Vaye-
nas; the student, Photis Paraskos; and the *saltadoros*, who is unnamed. Venezis is certainly correct when he describes the Greek
people as much tyrannized and truly wounded: of all nations in
Europe who fought the Germans (and none did so more nobly
than the Greeks), only Greece, for reasons mentioned above,
turned against her own Resistance and made monsters of her
heroes.

Although *Block C* went on to many performances, it had initial
difficulties both with casting and staging. The former problem is
dealt with at some length by Drassos Kastanakis in a review written for the *Free Press* (December 21, 1945). Both in the play and
in his previous works, according to Kastanakis, Venezis brought
true glory to Greek literature. The play was a worthy chronicle of
national Resistance to the "blond assassins." [9] The reading of the
play prior to its staging was, for the reviewer, one of the great
moments of his life. All those present, men of letters, of the
theater and of the arts, were greatly moved. Despite this auspi-
cious beginning, the staging of *Block C* was terrible—as if the
actors had set out to destroy the play.[10] Each player acted as if he
had just descended from his own separate star. Following their
individual whims, the players missed the whole depth of the play,
including the symbolic value of the Red Cross girl who passes and
says, "Courage." Kastanakis attacks especially the one who played
the *saltadoros* as an actor fit only for frothy plays of no substance.
Despite the folly of poor acting and miscasting, the National
Theater made progress toward professionalism. "It has given us
the most remarkable work till now, written by Elias Venezis." [11]

In a "Director's Note" prefacing the published version of *Block*

C (1946), Pellos Katsellis discusses the theatrical interpretation of the play and some of its staging problems. He notes that several commentators thought the work had many virtues as literature, but that it was not a play.[12] Katsellis and his theater associates disagreed. The director speculates that the main reason for the antinomy (between *Block C* as literature and as drama) is the humanity of the work, the author's love for his fellow man, given as a harvest of life and not of literature. When one has captured an excess of genuine life-drama, he is less likely to give all his attention to the conventional theatrical art, just as a real flood on its way to the sea from the mountains holds to previously made channels, but if such channels do not exist, the water makes its own. Thus a major canon of theatrical art is the need of the dramatist to conceive his theme plastically, creatively, and individually. And no matter what his treatment, he must remain true to the spirit of his theme, his imitation of nature.

A dramatist, Katsellis goes on, must attend to both the completeness and the genuineness of his theatrical composition. Had Venezis employed profuse esoteric action, crowded episodes, character clashes, and other elements of theatricality, he would have sacrificed the essence of dramatic art.[13] A play whose theme is the fate of seven doomed men facing death must divest itself of all extraneous activity to make its full impact. The implication is that Venezis refuses for the sake of spectacle to mar the more important integrity of the play as a play. The director, Katsellis, castigates the critics of *Block C* for not realizing that such elements as action and change of scene are the *means* and not the *ends* of dramatic creation.[14]

In his article Katsellis defends the play, the author, and the National Theater. On the other hand, he does recognize that the theatrical interpretation of the play, the staging, presented a number of difficulties. First, the combined problem of idealizing and individualizing the seven prisoners. They must be idealized because they are heroes, above the commonplace; therefore they must speak and act in an elevated and more perfect manner, and take the same license with the "natural" that language does when it transcends the literal to become poetic. Katsellis suggests a dramaturgy which best suits a play like *Block C*. He terms it poetic realism. Its successful realization depends upon the actor's ability to avoid all vulgar naturalistic qualities and all bombast in the declamation. Another problem is the need for each of the seven principals in *Block C* to remain constantly dynamic, in spirit, while before the audience. This necessary isolation, in dialogue and everything else, had to merge and combine into a totality that was the presentation. The director lists several special problems arising from this organic necessity: 1. the confined area of the cell in which a dynamic movement had to be staged; 2. the correct placement of the players on the stage so that at all times what they said was both clear and effective; 3. the proper arrangement of the cell where the action occurs. Above all, the presentation had to bring out the inner spiritual quality of the play.[15]

Before this interesting note on dramaturgical theory and its application to *Block C*, Venezis has his own note in which he expresses some of his feelings regarding both the imprisonment and his coming to write about it. He mentions the instinctive and mechanical reactions of men during the intensest moments of danger, when they are face to face with death. At such moments they feel most alone, isolated, when even their closest neighbors appear strange and unknown.[16] Venezis writes that he was an author of books who found himself in a difficult hour, in a German prison cell. "He was wrapped, as the air wraps the earth, in darkness and fear" (p. 12). While there he felt the desperate need for expression—as others had scratched their names, symbols, and other legends on the wall. Out of this desperation was born the idea of *Block C*. Perhaps he was fated for such a task, to leave a chronicle for posterity; the author's generation was one of the most unusual in history since it encompassed two world wars. "Perhaps it is our fate," Venezis writes, "to leave only chronicles" (p. 13). He refers to some of the staging problems which Katsellis also mentions. Finally, he says that *Block C*, the play of the Occupation, "was an offering to the pain which our fatherland experienced during the years of servitude, an offering to the exaltation before death shown by our people, and to their passion for freedom" (p. 14).

IV   *The Novel of the Occupation*

In the novel *Exodus*, published in 1950, Venezis returns to the theme of uprooted people passing through an unknown and perilous environment. They seek a sanctuary which tragically eludes them. Sub-titled the "Book of the Occupation," *Exodus* presents a rather limited segment of Greek experience during the war. It is, of course, the author's privilege to limit his scope to any degree he chooses. In this novel Venezis has chosen to bypass all the struggle against the Germans and to concentrate on a group of refugees, groping their way through enemy occupied territory, who are determined to reach Athens where they hope to find food and shelter. Again, as in *Block C* and other works, various character types are thrown together by chance and forced to share a common destiny. How they interact and what they endure constitute the movement and provide the suspense of the narrative. The way in which Venezis invokes the Greek tradition, the legendary past, enriches both the action, the characterization, and the thought. *Exodus* is an odyssey in a dangerous land where past and present merge, and echoes of ancient tragedies reinforce those of the present.

The novel is divided into three parts: "The Road," "Kithairon," and "Kolonos." Venezis has employed an opening similar to that of *Serenity* in which two smugglers of antiquities notice a column of strangers slowly moving ahead. In *Exodus* two women of Kastoria, returning home after gathering kindling wood, also notice a column below them. The time is winter, 1942, the darkest moment of Greek defeat. Burdened and afraid, the two women hurry to beat a sunset curfew. Snow covers the ground. The pack of about thirty refugees have come pursued and hungry all the way from Drama, in Thrace, where the Bulgarians invaded and slaughtered their people. At the hut of one of the women, a family of five refugees is to spend the night: the two grandparents, their daughter, and her two children. After describing the atrocities committed by the Bulgarians, the old woman warns, "They will come down here also. They will come down and destroy you. Your time will come." [17]

The Kastorian woman, named Anthi, must leave for Athens to find the husband who deserted her. She must do so immediately, for the Italians are rounding up all those like herself who offered the Thracians shelter. She and her two daughters join the family they housed. Thus begins the "exodus" under conditions that make the biblical symbolism inescapable—except that there is no God to help them and their Promised Land, Athens, is paralyzed with famine.

They spend the first night in a desolate chapel where "The water and the wind had eaten away the ikons of Byzantine saints"

(p. 36). They share the bread brought by Anthi. On the road heading south they luckily halt a truck driven by two Greek merchants taking bales of fur scraps to market. For the price of five thousand drachmas and a golden cross (supplied by Anthi) the drivers agree to take them to the outskirts of Athens. The refugees ride on the cargo—a cold and rough ride. The old man steals a boiled duck from Anthi's bag of belongings and devours much of it before he is discovered. They spend the night at inns in Kozani, and the next night in Elassona. The following day they pass a lovely snow-capped mountain which the driver says is Olympus, the ancient home of the gods. When the woman from Kastoria asks what is up there now, he replies, "Rocks. Hard rocks" (p. 60). Both the pagan and Christian gods have abandoned the refugees. It is raining when they reach Larissa, but they must sleep outside in the truck.

In the morning the grandfather goes off in the mist and returns with a bloody cat he has killed, and which he intends to boil and eat. On the road they run into a gory scene: the Italians have just slaughtered twenty Greek hostages for an act of sabotage. From the pile of corpses, a hostage miraculously rises and begins to flee. The furious Italians empty their rifles at him, but he escapes. To make up for the lost corpse, the Italians must kill someone from the truck. They reach in to grab one of the Thracian children, but his mother pulls him back. They next grab the grandfather, and this time the mother (his daughter) helps to push him out to die instead of her youngster. Had the old man not delayed them for the cat, they might have completely avoided the danger. They save the dead cat.

Grief-stricken, the refugees ride on until they meet up with a herd of about two hundred sick and lame donkeys. The animals will be eaten in Athens where famine is rampant. Again the refugees are stopped, this time by a rock rolled onto the road by a gaunt stranger who claims to be from the oracle of Delphi on Parnassus. He speaks in a seemingly oracular manner, insane and cryptic. He wants to lead them for safety to the lion's den. "At some time we shall become eagles" (p. 79). The lion is a statue, the Lion of Chaeronea, standing in a grove of cypress trees. It remains changeless despite the flux of time and man's fate. That night, while they boil the cat, the refugees learn the tragedy of Pantazis, the madman of Delphi. The Germans had arrived in

Delphi searching for hidden guns, but there were none. To get Pantazis, who knew nothing, to confess, they pushed his two young sons off a cliff to their death. Since then he roams about to help people become eagles. Had his sons been eagles, they would have flown to safety.

Near ancient Thebes, where the truck breaks down, Anthi goes for a walk during which she meets a girl who has kept vigil for four days beneath a hanged man, her brother. Her other brother is already buried, but this one has been left hanging. The parallel with the myth is obvious. The Germans, in forbidding his burial, assume the role of King Kreon. Polyneikes has been hanged in order to terrify the Thebans. His brother, Eteokles, has been buried. The Germans had caught them while trying to escape to Egypt. Thus the girl is a modern Antigone; and though she has no real sister like Ismene, Anthi takes on the part by deciding, in defiance of the enemy, to help this Antigone bury her Polyneikes. On his chest is a sign that reads, "Whoever dares to touch him will be shot" (p. 124).

Soon after the two women bury the hanged man, a German motorcyclist arrives to check on the situation. He roars off to make his report. The women hurry back to the stalled truck which they know they must leave. The refugees flee up the mountainside, and with them goes the Theban girl. The mountain on which they happen to be is Kithairon. In the mythical past, the baby Oedipus was brought there to die in the hope of averting a horrible fate.

Part Two of *Exodus*, entitled "Kithairon," goes back in time to April, 1941, to pick up the story of two characters whose destiny eventually merges with that of the pilgrims from the north. They are the condemned but innocent youth Gregou and the admitted murderer Panagos. Both are in prison when they escape during an air raid that destroys the building. The background of Gregou is given. While pregnant with him during the Catastrophe of 1922, his mother luckily escapes to Lesbos where he is born. He grows up in an orphanage. One night he takes part in a drunken brawl which leaves one man dead. Although innocent, Gregou is convicted and sent to prison where he meets Panagos. After their escape, they travel the road of the refugees. There they hear a massive clamor of people and motors ahead. They climb to avoid whatever monstrous thing is coming, and they see from a lofty vantage the Greek Army and countless civilians, fleeing in panic before the Germans and Italians. Stukas dive bomb and strafe the road. "The road was death, all ran in hope of avoiding the fate of the road" (p. 177). In the spring of 1941, the convicts arrive on Mount Kithairon.

They find work with an old woodsman who lives with his sickly wife. The man's only son (sired by another man) has been killed in Albania. The woodsman's wife dies, admitting on her deathbed the truth about her infidelity. The old man, stunned and embittered, curses his wife's memory. He turns evil. When the first snow falls, he orders Panagos to visit the hut of Constantine Tsellas and ask for the return of a loan. Angry, the murderer wants to kill the woodsman, rob him of his gold, and thus assure their safety. He also hopes to implicate Gregou.

At the hut of Tsellas the wife tells Panagos that her sick husband has gone to Livadia. She has a baby. A bearded blond man arrives whom the woman tries to palm off as a mute. Actually, he is a New Zealander who has made a separate peace for himself and now lives with her. Panagos returns empty-handed to the old woodsman who sees happening to Tsellas what also happened to him: an unfaithful wife has taken a lover. Maddened by the new evil, the woodsman vows to kill the woman; at about the same time the convict Panagos vows to kill the woodsman. The old man leaves. He says he has business down in Thebes.

A couple of days later the woodsman wakes early and gives both Gregou and Panagos duties (tending goats and cutting wood) that would get them out of the way. Panagos suspects that something is up. Instead of going off to the forest, he returns to the hut ostensibly to get his flint for smoking. He sees a patrol of ten Italians trudging up the trail. The truth dawns on him; the old woodsman had gone to Thebes to betray the New Zealander. Now a great peril approaches the lovers. First, the Italian patrol. A safe distance behind, the woodsman. And last of all, the murderer Panagos.

Events move fast. As the New Zealander steps outside the door to bring in wood, the Italians open fire; he runs in and shoots back with a revolver. Both he and the Greek girl are killed. When the Italians stop firing, they hear only the baby's cries. They leave the door ajar so wild animals can enter to devour the child. Having watched from behind a knoll, the woodsman enters the hut when the Italians depart. There he curses the dead lovers whose blood mingles on the floor. At this point Panagos also enters the hut. He has a knife. In the ensuing fight the woodsman bashes in the murderer's head with his sturdy staff. He keeps bashing until the staff is covered with brains and blood; then he runs off leaving the baby with the three corpses.

Not until the next day, and after much badgering, does the woodsman tell Gregou that he saw some Italians heading for the hut of Tsellas. Hurrying, Gregou reaches the death house, sees the three bodies, and finds the baby crying. Much shaken, he wraps the baby in a scarf and runs back to the woodsman's hut. He nearly trips over a bloody staff but hardly notices it. He boils goat's milk and feeds the baby. Suddenly, he hears footsteps outside. The refugees from the road, fleeing to avoid the penalty of having buried the hanged man, arrive for shelter at the hut. "Who are you?" Gregou asks, and he looks into the eyes of the girl from Thebes.

The third part of *Exodus*, "Kolonos," refers obviously to *Oedipus at Kolonos*, the last play in the Sophoclean trilogy, when Oedipus finally reaches serenity—semi-divine, purged of the old curse, and sacredly honored, when he dies, by the hospitable and law-loving Athenians. However, one cannot draw the parallel too closely. No character in *Exodus* is the modern equivalent of Oedipus. Nor is there, for that matter, a protagonist on whose fate the reader concentrates throughout. At first the emphasis is on the woman from Kastoria, but then it shifts to Gregou, the condemned but innocent convict. One finds, however, coincidence of geography. At this legendary place, at another time, certain tragedies occurred whose immensity has touched the deepest part of man; and here and now, in this war, similar tragedies are happening once more.

Exodus ends with the pilgrims reaching "a place that is called Kolonos." This final stage of the journey begins at the hut of the old woodsman on Mount Kithairon, where Gregou now provides shelter and food for the refugees. He introduces himself to the girl from Thebes by his first name, Manolis. She is Angela, which in Greek means "angel." Slowly the natural and inevitable occurs: an idyll of love on Mount Kithairon between the two condemned youths. She explains why she can never return to Thebes. "Thebes kills," she says. Both believe in old superstitions, those analogous to the prophecies in *Oedipus Rex*. His fate, he believes, is associated with a cypress tree, and they pass such a tree when they climb to the heights above the hut. As for Angela, a fortune teller once told her that her destiny would be a man with a mark of the sea upon him. And indeed Manolis Gregou has such a mark on his arm, the tattoo of a Gorgon rising above the ocean waves. The Gorgon carries a basket in which lies a baby. Beyond the water as a symbol of earth stands a tall cypress. Thus the preordained fates of Manolis and Angela merge and grow fast on Mount Kithairon.

Climbing high, the couple find a cave just as a storm breaks in fury. During the rain a fierce thunderbolt strikes nearby and briefly blinds Gregou (a hint of Oedipus); and when they look out they see that his symbolic cypress has been split down the middle. They regard this as luck, for they could have remained under the tree and died from the bolt. In the cave, on the wall, are legends from the past that memorialize the role of Mount Kithairon in the affairs of man. Included are vignettes about a Persian, a Norman of the Crusades, an Albanian in a war against the Turks, and so on. Now in this cave, on this mountain, Gregou and the girl from Thebes are learning about each other while the rain turns into a cataract and three bodies still lie unburied at the hut of Tsellas.

For his own safety Gregou must find out how and why his comrade Panagos died. Therefore, he returns, this time with Angela, to the scene of the dead. He remembers the bloody staff and where he saw it, but it is gone. At the hut, however, he and Angela came upon a weird sight: beside the three corpses, keeping vigil over them, is the old woodsman with the staff in his hand. He has gone insane.

Gregou decides to join the pilgrimage to Athens. They take the baby, of course, and a goat capable of giving milk. Like Oedipus, the baby had been left on Kithairon to die. After two days on the road the refugees arrive at what they take to be the environs of Athens. They knock on the first door, and a man who is dying of hunger lets them in. "What do they call this place?" asks Anthi, the woman from Kastoria, and the man's wife replies, "Kolonos. Here they call it Kolonos" (p. 357).

V   A Critique

The novel *Exodus* is the last major endeavor of Venezis to chronicle the cruelty, blindness, and tragedy of war. He chose a period, early 1942, with a flashback to April, 1941, when the Greek people had not yet made their heroic Resistance felt. They had organized, however, the National Liberation Front, or EAM, which was officially launched on September 27, 1941.[18] Thus it may be somewhat unhistorical for the refugees not to have met a single partisan in all their journey down from Macedonia and Thessaly—areas rugged enough to sustain the underground struggle. In the hard non-military and non-political situation, the social distress, the terror, *Exodus* is certainly authentic and stark. Of this period the eminent historian of the Balkans, Professor L.S. Stavrianos, writes: "The first winter of the occupation had taught Greece a lesson. German inflation destroyed the financial workings of the country. German looting stripped it clean. German reprisals slaughtered ten Greeks for every German. Famine tortured all Greece, and in Athens and Piraeus carts made daily trips to clear away emaciated corpses." [19] Venezis' novel illustrates well the fundamental belief of the author that the Greeks are much tyrannized and deeply wounded, that this has been their fate.

In terms of art, *Exodus* exemplifies a number of literary strategies which Venezis has found successful in writing the popular Greek novel, in the demotic, intended to reach a maximum audience in a country where illiteracy still abounds. Where no large stable and educated middle class exists, an author either tries to write for the elite (as does George Seferis), or he writes for the masses, in more or less their own speech, as do Kazantzakis, Myrivilis, and Venezis. Even among the demotic writers, however, there can exist a rather wide level of language, from the quite formal to very near the vulgate, or the *malliari,* as the Greeks call it. In fiction such as *Exodus,* Venezis uses a very informal diction aimed at unsophisticated readers whom too many abstractions, complexities, and subtleties might confuse. He is not a bookish scholar-writer, although he is personally learned; instead, he is a modern folk writer. For his themes, characters, and diction he goes directly to the people—not to those who have read Darwin, Marx, Freud, or Sartre, but to the "poor devils" of land and sea, mountain and plain. These *foukarades* live by simple inherited

logic, by signs and superstitions, by resignation to fate, and by
natural instincts. They have stolid endurance but, as Venezis depicts them, they have little humor and less wit.

In the lives of simple folk nothing is more dramatic in actuality
than great historic events that terrorize, starve, uproot, pursue,
enslave, wound, and kill them. The residual impact of these
events, especially defeat in war, automatically contributes feeling,
suspense, and meaning to the limited action that becomes the
plot, for example, of a novel like *Exodus.* The larger event, in fact,
assumes the formidable shape of *moira,* of fate, for those who are
caught in its cruel imperatives. The external pressures on them
remain so constant and overwhelming that very little use is ever
made of their inner conflicts, moral or otherwise, as added means
of motivation. Venezis rarely allows the reader to experience their
inner consciousness. They are trapped by their fate in a vast predicament; to all the ups and downs that it brings them they react
in accordance with the need. The author, being in command, can
manage both the events and the reactions in order to achieve the
greatest dramatic effect.

This management runs the risk of being artifice and not art
when the result tends to be melodrama and not genuine tragedy.
Tragedy derives from dynamic characters who have acted, at least
in part, from strong internal pressures that involve moral choice.
Only melodrama can result from the actions of essentially static
characters, typed to fit a theme, no matter how dreadful their ulti-
mate fate. The violent scenes on Mount Kithairon are melodra-
matic, even gothic: three corpses strewn about the bloody hut
with a helpless baby, crying and alone, left overnight to the mercy
of the wolves. The tears of the reader flow, no doubt, if the reader
is sentimental enough and not distressed by the contrived staging
of the scenes. While the baby cries among the bodies, the old
woodsman walks off cold to its fate just as the Italian killers had
done before him. No doubt the woodsman is as evil as the fascists,
but it would take a most puritanical reader, Greek or otherwise, to
accept as sufficient motivation for his bloodthirsty deeds the fact
that the wife of Tsellas (no relation to him) has taken a lover
(her husband being sick and infertile) with whom she has conceived a child. No doubt, too, the Greek peasant is quite medieval
in his views on sex, chastity, and fidelity, particularly as they
affect women. Nevertheless, unless the reader is himself so back-

ward and merciless, or unless he takes the woodsman for granted as a predictable type, he is likely to regard the gothic mountain scenes as the result not of profound characterization but of the more superficial needs of plot.

Despite these considerations, *Exodus* has many poignant moments, including many insights into character, that qualify it as one of the better Greek stories about the Second World War. Its refusal to complicate the characters with the actual ideologies that both united and divided the Greeks during the German Occupation (between Right and Left, monarchist and republican) allows the author the freedom to deal with his characters at the most primitive level of existence. They are universal in time and place. They are Jews in flight from Egypt, they are ancient Athenians and Spartans retreating before the Persian hordes.

Uncomplicated though the types may be, their predicament has anything but a simple solution. Their country is in the enemy's hands. The enemy starves, tortures, and kills Greek men, women, and children. He kills ten Greek hostages for every dead German. Man's first duty on this earth is to survive. For many of earth's "poor devils," existence is precarious enough, given the reluctance of nature in such lands as Greece to provide an adequate bounty. But when to this natural antagonist is added a monstrously cruel *human* one, an Occupation army, then the "poor devils" such as the refugees in *Exodus* must rely upon a grasping, furtive animal-like cunning and courage in order to endure. Venezis expertly dramatizes the perils, both those known and unknown, that harass the refugees on the road toward their dubious haven in Athens.

The play *Block C* and the novel *Exodus*, as indicated, are the author's major efforts to chronicle the agony of Greece during the German Occupation. In setting they reflect extremes: the action of the former occurs in a small enclosure, a prison cell, while that of the latter is the open country, the mountains of Macedonia and Thessaly, the perilous road to Athens.

Were these the only works by Venezis on the war, they would still be a creditable achievement of a writer, gentle by nature, whose integrity compels him to depict man's inhumanity to man. His allusions to the biblical exodus of the Jews from Egypt and the classical myths of Antigone and Oedipus support his view that tragedy, due in great measure to man's own evil, has been the perennial fate of the Greek people. That he does allow for hope is again illustrated in *Exodus* when love begins on Mount Kithairon for the condemned youths, whose destined paths cross there, for Gregou, the "sea-touched" innocent, and for Angela, the Theban girl. Despite the general chaos, they have each other now as well as the rescued baby (a symbol of life's continuity) with which to face whatever lies ahead in the famine-ridden city. Together with the wartime short stories already examined here and those to be examined, *Block C* and *Exodus* constitute on the part of Venezis a significant literary reaction to the drama of war.

CHAPTER 5

The Later Stories

I Wartime

THE short stories in *Wartime*, published in 1946, are unified by the theme of war.[1] As in *Number 31328* and other works, war does not ennoble man; it brutalizes him. Venezis does not see any spectacular heroics in killing. War's deeds are barbaric. They deserve no praise. *Wartime* focuses on the people who remain civilized and humane despite the savagery.

The first of its two sections is entitled "Wartime"; the second, "Anna's Book." In the first are six short stories and three accounts, "Chronicle of 1940," "Chronicle of 1942," and "Calendar." These three are diary-like narratives of the events of World War II, interspersed with personal impressions, reactions, and experiences. "Anna's Book" consists of six stories, most of which deal with the growth and awareness of the little girl Anna in wartime conditions. Occasionally sentimental and repetitive, and sometimes marred by trite treatment of events and emotions, these stories do not equal "People of the Saroniko" and "Tourkolimano" of the first section. The dedication of *Wartime* reads: "To the youth of the world, of my country, of our allies, and of our enemies, who fell in Greece, sacrificed to the barbarism of war."

In the story "People of the Saroniko," Barba Philip, with his son and daughter, lives on an island owned by a rich man. Donkey's Island is barren and comfortless. Not even the hunters who come to shoot quail and pheasants can bear to spend the night there. Fotini, Barba Philip's daughter, views the island as a shrine. Poseidon's ruins and the story of Christ are intermingled for the fourteen year old girl. No evil can touch the island, for it is sacred.

When the Italian soldiers come to search the island for partisans, Barba Philip sends the girl up into the mountain to join his son, the young shepherd. On the way down she loops around her waist the rope used to lead the donkey. A fat Italian officer, to impress her, shoots his pistol near the donkey's ear. Terrified, the

animal crazily runs down the trail, dragging the girl. Barba Philip
finds her dead. Although he has never known hatred, he begins to
long for revenge. Later, as he is about to kill a sleeping Italian
with a rock, he sees a flock of wildly cawing crows circling above.
Startled, he exclaims, "My God, what was I about to do?" [2] He
awakens the soldier and sends him away.

He begins to ponder the meaning of life. He remembers that he
never saw his mother smile, nor his wife. Fotini had not lived long
enough to smile. Barba Philip thinks that perhaps death is better
than life. The riddle of living is somewhat clarified for him by a
scene he witnesses. As a gull comes up from the sea with a fish in
its bill, a crow tries to wrest it away. Once, the gull wins, but
another time the crow flies away with the fish. So Barba Philip
sees life as a struggle in which gulls can become crows and crows
can become gulls.

When the Italians surrender, a German ship carrying two thousand Italian prisoners is sunk by a British submarine. An Italian
corpse floats to the island shores, and Barba Philip and his son
find it. In hatred they send it out to sea, but it floats back. Once
again, they push it out, and the son takes the cross from the dead
soldier's neck. Greek divers, seeking the oil in the hold of the German ship, have come upon two thousand standing corpses. The
sea has not decayed them; they remain accursed, crying for earth
to cover them. That night, when Barba Philip and his son visit the
seashore, they sight the corpse again. This time Barba Philip has it
buried under the pine next to his wife's grave.

The war over, the young hunters come again, accompanied by a
girl. Finding a skull and thigh bone that presumably belonged to
one of the drowned victims, she summons the young hunters.
They toss the skull about. Fixing the skull on a stick, the girl urges
the hunters to shoot at it. When Barba Philip sees them, he wildly
sends them away. "Are you then not afraid of anything?" he asks.
"And looking like Fate, blood and tears intermingled, his hair
streaming, he sends them away: 'Away from our grief'" (p. 61).

The old man and his son bury the skull and thigh bone in a
third grave under the pine. Barba Philip digs a shallow hole in the
second grave and there buries the cross which his son had saved.
"Let it be with him," he murmurs. "It was all he had" (p. 62).
Then he cries in grief, "My child!" His son asks him in astonish-

ment, "Do you grieve for the Italian?" The old man simply responds again mournfully, "My child" (p. 63).

Thus Barba Philip is forever rid of hatred. Never can he be a
crow. Always he is the seagull, free and great of heart. All the
war's youthful dead are his children. His daughter's death is
senseless but war, too, is senseless. He cannot deny burial to the
corpse of the enemy, for that would be the final inhumanity. If
there is no hope for the humanizing of the young hunters and the
girl, there is much hope for Philip's son, the young shepherd. The
boy grieves because he cannot remember the face of the Italian
soldier whose corpse was washed up on the shores of Donkey's
Island. All he can recall is that it was a young and beardless face.

The issue of the story seems to be whether the way of the crow
or that of the seagull will triumph. Barba Philip exemplifies this
conflict and its outcome in his realization of his own and the
enemy's humanity. Venezis sketches his character broadly. Since
the old man is simple and uneducated, he is not much given to
complex introspection. Venezis shifts the point of view of the
story to accommodate Barba Philip's character. The first part is
omniscient; but the events which occur after the death of Barba
Philip's daughter are filtered largely through the old man's consciousness. The reader hence is brought nearer the old man and
comes to know his mind much more intimately.

The structure of the story is quite loose, and events occur only
as a result of chance (in this case, the war) and not because the
probabilities of the story so demand. The incidents are chosen
deliberately to illustrate the theme of the story. For this reason the
characters are generalized. The young hunters are the crows, de-
riving pleasure from the victory of the kill. The fat Italian officer
whose joke kills the young girl is a crow. The young girl coming
with the hunters after the war should be sensitive and humane.
Instead, she is broadly drawn as corrupted by the values of city
life, a mocker of Barba Philip, and moved to insane hatred by the
sight of the Italian skull. The characters of the story are symbolic
of good or evil. Even the physical description of the young shepherd is scanty. We know only that what his father does will make
the boy a seagull or a crow.

The daughter Fotini we meet while she is still alive. Venezis
pauses to peer into Fotini's (her name means "the bright one")

young mind. He makes us feel her exultant happiness in being alive, her love for the donkey whose wild flight kills her, her strong faith in the goodness of Christ and Poseidon, and her untroubled confidence that all will be well in the end. Fotini represents all the young victims in the story. Her thoughts stand for the thoughts of all youth that must be sacrificed to the war. For this reason Venezis must show them to us. We do not need to learn about the thoughts of those who are crows; their actions are sufficient for us to recognize them.

The language is simple. Venezis uses the short sentence, understatement, and the poetic and unsophisticated diction of the Greek shepherd and peasant.

TOURKOLIMANO—"Tourkolimano" is the story of a different war, that in a man's soul. The issue is whether a man can avert his fate without sacrificing his inner peace. The answer is an uncompromising no.

Captain Vasili has given up sailing the seas to work in the city mills. He and his family still live near the docks and the beach in Tourkolimano. When there is little work in the mills, Captain Vasili sits and watches the building of the fishing boats. In his eyes there is a wild and distant look. He had three times sailed beyond the Gulf of the Saroniko and lost three boats. "Three boats are enough to pay in one lifetime." [3] Captain Vasili grows bitter with this thought as the years pass. With him, his wife, and two sons lives Barba Stavro, a one-armed fisherman of about fifty. The story opens with Barba Stavro bringing home a seagull. The gull's feathers have been plucked for lures by a fisherman, and Barba Stavro buys the bird out of pity. He pays a great price, his entire day's catch of fish. The seagull will replace another named Johnny which, during a famine, Captain Vasili had killed to save one of his sons from starvation.

At first, the captured gull cries painfully when he watches the other gulls dip into the sea for fish and wheel about in the skies. Barba Stavro grieves for the land enslavement of the gull. Since its feathers have not grown enough, he cannot release it yet to fly over the seas. Refusing to believe that the fisherman intends to release the bird, Captain Vasili taunts Barba Stavro. The gull, as always in Venezis a benign symbol, has been rescued by Barba Stavro and is associated with him. Captain Vasili, who has rejected his destiny, the sea, is an embittered, poisoned man. He taunts and mocks the honest and simple Barba Stavro out of envy. Barba Stavro, who knows the sea's magic, its peace and terror, is like his own seagull. The captain is in contrast guileful, corroded with hatred, and crowlike.

When the time comes for a new fishing boat to be launched, Barba Stavro happily tells Captain Vasili and his sons that Johnny the seagull will sail with the boat. The vessel's captain has agreed to free the bird on a distant island. On the eve of the launching Captain Vasili pulls out the gull's feathers and sneaks off to spend the night and dawn on the western side of Tourkolimano away from the sight of the launching. His curiosity and gnawing desire bring him to where the crowds are gathered to watch the blessing of the fishing boat. There, Barba Stavro accuses him sadly of pulling the bird's feathers.

In the meantime, Johnny the seagull, confused by the crowds and awkward without his feathers, gets his leg caught under the boat sliding into the waters. The boat must move only forward, despite the bird, otherwise there will be bad luck. Barba Stavro protests that the bird's foot will be torn off. Then Captain Vasili takes out his knife and slays the gull, reddening the boat with its blood. He cuts the leg away from the gull and lays the dead Johnny on the sand.

"A good omen," cry the women. "The gull's blood on the boat is good."

"From the past, from the mythical age of Greece," says Venezis, "comes the ancestral memory of the blood sacrifice to the gods" (pp. 115–16).

Captain Vasili returns to his house. There, his two boys have buried the gull on a promontory where Johnny used to gaze at the sea. Dazedly, Captain Vasili makes the picture of a boat over the burial mound with pebbles. It is the kind of boat he lost the last time he sailed.

"Tourkolimano" highlights the conflict between a man and his destiny. Captain Vasili has given up the sea, but the sea will not give him up. It dominates his every action. Vasili's struggle to change his fate twists his life. Symbolically, he enslaves Johnny the seagull by pulling out the bird's feathers. Yet, for the bird as for himself, Captain Vasili's act means death. Just as he slays the landbound bird, so has he slain himself. His deathstone is the lost fishing boat made of pebbles that he designs over the gull's burial mound.

Venezis is very effective when he deals with thwarted characters like Captain Vasili. His omniscient point of the view enables him to draw them unsentimentally and with simple strokes. Captain Vasili never analyzes himself; he simply acts. Because he challenges fate he must be unhappy. Happiness is only for those who submit. Barba Stavro accepts his sea heritage; the sea has taken his arm, but the sea has also given him peace.

As Venezis' characters are unsophisticated and unsentimentalized, so is the language of the story. Simple and touching, the short sentences quicken the pace. As always, Venezis must pause to create a special atmosphere. To show us Barba Stavro's imaginative conception of the sea world, he has him tell the story of the Gorgon who eternally searches for her brother. The tale serves to intensify Captain Vasili's conflict and underscore his struggle to escape the sea. As such, it is a unifying device in the loose plot. The romantic fable buttresses the realism of the story. Most modern Greek tales are combinations of myth and history, gentleness and terror. They are still told by the Barbas, the old uncles, whose age has often given them wisdom and humble resignation to things as they must be.

THE OTHER STORIES—The other stories in the collection are unified by the war theme. "The Old Woman of Lamia" is about an aged grandmother who finds a wounded Greek youth, the only survivor of a German massacre. Not only does she nurse him back to health, but she determines to cross the mountains (which she has never before longed to do) to help him get back to his fellow guerrilla fighters. Although a traveler had once told her that in those mountains great history was made at a pass named Thermopylae, she had no desire to leave her village. Now, to get the young partisan past the German soldiers, she loads him in her cart with twigs and wood and reaches those mountains. Venezis does not attend her bravery with fanfare. Like the other fighters in his stories, she sees her actions as her destiny, to which she wonderingly submits.

Three selections consist of journal entries, "The Chronicle of 1940," "The Chronicle of 1942," and "Calendar." They show the narrator's individual reaction to personal incidents and national and local war events.

The last part of *Wartime,* "Anna's Book," is concerned with the birth of the narrator's daughter and sketches her growth and development. Although her mother tries to shelter her from knowing the deprivation and brutality of war, Anna learns. In "A Dead Bird," when she and her mother go on March twenty-fifth, Greek Independence Day, to place a commemorative wreath at the statues of the heroes of the Revolution of 1821, they see other children doing the same. The German soldiers come and begin to shoot. All escape but three. When Anna goes to look at the blood and the trampled wreaths, she finds a dead white bird shattered by bullets. Digging a hole in the soil of the park, she buries the bird and puts yellow flowers on the burial mound. And so, the child buries peace, the gentle white bird, the peace of nations, and the peace of her childhood.

Wartime suffers from moments of creative fatigue. The accounts of the war, as represented in the chronicles and "Calendar," are ineffective. They fail to move. The stories included here in "Anna's Book" are not well developed. All obviously didactic, they abound in shadowy characters, excessive narrative, and insufficient action. Anna is never a real girl; she is an airy and romantic conception. While the stories strive to show the effect of war on the very young, none in this Anna series are as effective as "The Broken Branch" (1943) which appears in *The Defeated.* The best story, "Tourkolimano," only mentions the war. "People of the Saroniko," a good story, is drawn out and its lesson and symbols are too repetitive and obvious. Venezis misses the suggestive quality of his earlier stories. Too often he forthrightly *tells* us what dramatic action *shows* us in his earlier works.

None of his characters actually come to grips with the reality of war as did the narrator of *Number 31328* or even, in a lesser way, the characters of *Block C.* The old grandmother in "The Old Woman of Lamia" is one of his better characters. But Venezis does not succeed generally in bringing to life the tragic zeal of the Greek people in fighting and resisting the enemy in World War II.

II   The Defeated

The Defeated is divided into two sections, stories of Greece and
stories of the distant world. Most of the stories are quite short;
some can more properly be called sketches or anecdotes.[4] The
exception is "Theonichos and Mnisarete," which reappears in this
volume. All show characters who, in one way or another, have
been trapped or defeated by life. Most have come to terms with
their defeat and have learned to accept it quietly. Some still struggle: for them there is no *yalini*, no peace.

NIGHT OF ASKLEPIOS—"Night of Asklepios" tells about Ahmet,
the guide to the ruins of the temple of Asklepios in Cos. A simple
man, he loves the ruins and those who show reverence towards
them. The latter he takes to his wife, Babante, who reads their
palms. Both she and Ahmet grieve when she sees death for some
but does not reveal it. That fall, when the tourists stop coming,
Ahmet suddenly decides to ask his wife to look into his palm and
tell him when his hour will come. She refuses, alarmed that he
should ask. But for both, the great human terror of death has
come and sleep is forever shattered.

The guide is a recurring character. Venezis shows the irony of
his personal fear of death even as he cherishes the dead and lives
among them. Again, the notion is suggested that in Greece man
cannot avert his face from death. The ruins of the dead past are a
pointed reminder of man's mortality. Neither the theme nor the
characters are new for Venezis.

THE TWO WOMEN AND THE TOWER—In "The Two Women and
the Tower" the narrator is a tourist on Andros. In a historic castle
or tower once fortified against island invaders live a young Greek
girl and an Englishwoman. The girl guides the tourists through
the tower. She tells of an incident in which the women of Andros,
their men away, took refuge in the fort against marauding pirates.
By a trick they deceived the pirates into believing that only old
women were within the walls. The girl clearly loves the tower.
But the Englishwoman sits alone in the dark reading *A Midsum-
mer Night's Dream,* having renounced but not forgotten "the native land, that other sky, leaden and foggy." When she is asked
how she feels about her life in the tower, she replies "later and

with a faintly tremulous voice, 'I am happy.' It would have been unbearable to be pitied." [5]

This can more properly be called an account, a travel experience. The characters have possibilities which are undeveloped. Venezis poses the incongruity of the Englishwoman reading Shakespeare in the historic tower at Andros. Imprisoned forever here, trapped by unknown compulsions, the two women become sources of wonder for the reader. Venezis captures the ghost-laden atmosphere and bathes the women in its aura. However, the reader never knows enough because the work remains simply an impression.

TRAVEL ACCOUNTS—The travel accounts, both of which appeared in *Nea Estia*, focus on similar central figures, people removed from reality and wedded to the past. Venezis plumbed this possibility more extensively in "Theonichos and Mnisarete." He treats the same theme again in a sketch called "The Shadows of Phaistos." [6] Alexander Venetikos, who has been written about by Henry Miller, is the guide at the Minoan ruins of the palace at Phaistos. For Venetikos the ruins are life, and Venezis evokes the sadness of an illusory life spent among shadows.

In "The Old Man of the Seine and the Three" the narrator-tourist visits The Palace of Justice in Paris. The guide, an old man, shows him the cells of Andrea Chenier, Robespierre, and Marie Antoinette. Speaking of them as if alive, he observes: "I mix them up. They are one—unified by space and pain." [7]

THE BROKEN BRANCH—Another theme that Venezis exploits is that of the loss of innocence and the knowledge of hatred. In "The Broken Branch," the three-year-old Anna is protected by her parents from the war horrors of hunger, torture, and pain. The bombings and air battles are described for her as the play of the iron birds in the sky; the many-colored light-bursts of death as splendid fireworks. One day, while walking in the park, Anna and her mother watch a ragged, thin, and dark four-year-old boy play with pebbles. Failing to see the truck driving by, he strikes it with one of his pebbles. The driver, a Nazi soldier, gets out and silently drags the boy to the truck. Holding the boy's hand against the car, he coldly slams the door on it, breaking the hand. Throwing the boy down, the soldier leaves. "And the boy's moan became unbearable anguish; the leaves hushed, the bitter trees of the park bent, the good deities that attend men, they say, awoke to see. The boy with the eyes of the Aegean stood in the middle of the street moaning; and his hand hung ruined like a broken branch." [8] At Christmastime, when her parents gift Anna with a doll, the doll's chipped hand breaks. Anna's cries will not be stilled: "From now on every broken branch, every violent moment will remind her that evil springs from the hands of men. So Anna slowly will begin to understand men, slowly will begin to hate them. Such is the irreparable fate of all the children of wartime" (p. 47).

THE KNIFE OF BATAAN AND THE VERSES—Venezis here shows the spiritual loss that war brings about. A young man, aged and embittered in spirit, tells how his father and grandfather of eighty were executed by the German invaders. Seeking revenge, he began to fight the enemy at fourteen and finally saw the man who killed his relatives judged by a military court and executed. He recounts that he asked the German soldier how it felt to kill. The soldier replied, "You don't know how it feels to spill the blood of men; you don't know what seizes you so that you want to spill more and more." [9] The war over now, the boy reads and writes poetry. But this is not easy, "Because during the years I should have been taking afternoon strolls in the park with my tutor, I was learning how to kill" (p. 64). As the boy recites his poetry, he plays with a knife. "I love knives," he explains. "I understand knives. The Americans had this kind on Bataan" (pp. 64-5).

Venezis laments the loss of youthful innocence in this boy, who is poetically inclined, who loves poetry and, paradoxically, knives. Born of the war, his love for knives, instruments of death, coexists with his deep feeling for that poetry which celebrates love and life. Among the listening tourists is a mother who begins to weep. "Her tears were for this boy, for all the boys, who were not permitted when it was time to live joyfully, to be carefree, to know love and beauty. Instead, men's deeds put youth into furnaces; they shoved them into furnaces. And they burned them" (p. 64).

THE BANDIT PANCHO VILLA—As we have already seen, a favorite theme of Venezis is that of the uprooted or displaced. In a fine sketch called "The Bandit Pancho Villa," Peter, a Long Island farmer, "who keeps the color of the Icarian sky in his blue eyes," tells his story.[10] Enlisting in the army during the American inter-vention in Mexico in 1917, Peter helps to suppress Pancho Villa's insurrection. When he is asked his reason for going to war, Peter replies: "You fought Pancho Villa and ate. Better to eat and be killed than to die laying tracks for the Southern Pacific" (p. 139).

For Peter, Pancho Villa is a symbol of cruelty and inhuman exploitation. Recounting his experiences as an immigrant, he tells how a Greek Pancho Villa sold fellow Greeks to the railroad and another worked him all day for ten dollars a month, which was never paid. Pancho Villa is an Irish cook who beat and fired him because he did not understand a request; he is the Southern Pacific railroad, buying and tagging Peter and other immigrants "who, while laying tracks, left their bones in the deserts deep in-land" (p. 140). At the end of his account, Peter, proudly survey-ing his farm, remarking on his children and his wife, turns to the listener and asks, "Have I then triumphed over Pancho Villa?" The answer is silence. "Pancho Villa for each of us means the ulti-mate triumph: for none of us knows if we have conquered Pancho Villa or he has conquered us" (p. 146).

Peter not only represents the uprooted man, but also the one whose battle to conquer the Pancho Villa of the spirit testifies to the worthiness of humanity.

THE IMMIGRANT OF GRAND CANYON—In this sketch, Tony Karson has lost forever the country of his birth, but he is the first Greek to have vanquished the Grand Canyon. From Tripolitsa he came to open a restaurant high over the Grand Canyon. Elated at meeting a Greek tourist in America, Tony invites him to his mountain cabin. He talks about his home in Albuquerque, and the Greek tourist meets Tony's arthritic wife of English descent and their twelve-year-old son who knows no Greek. "How sad, how painful are the uprooted," observes the tourist on his visit to Tony's cabin.[11] Like his friend the Hopi Indian far from his people, Tony seems to be dolefully lonely. "When you return to Greece," he im-plores the visitor, "write it in the papers, perhaps announce it on the radio: 'I found Tony Karson, that is, Karkazis, from Tripolitsa. He lives and grows old on the Grand Canyon with his friend the Hopi Indian.' Do you hear?" (p. 132). Tony has arranged for an-other Greek to operate the restaurant at Grand Canyon when he dies, for the Greeks must continue here since Tony was the first.

The final sadness of estrangement occurs when Tony, listening to the roar of the Colorado River, says: "Everywhere that roar is the same." And later, "It reminds me of my village in the mountains of the Morea" (p. 133).

A FINN IN ALGIERS—This fine travel sketch shows us the more usual kind of character in *The Defeated*. The outcast Finn, who is also a character in the novel *The Ocean*, has achieved nothing, has lost everything. The *Captain Papazoglou*, a freighter, docks at Algiers to load a cargo of oil. The narrator describes the vendors who come aboard to sell their wares. Four prostitutes then come to entice the seamen, who have been ordered not to leave the ship. When the women dance provocatively, some of the men leap onto the dock and go off nearby with the women. After the men return, a drunken Finn appears, attended by a silent Algerian. Stranded in Algiers because he had been drinking and missed his own ship, the Finn pleads with the crew to take him aboard. Instead, they violently refuse, heaping on him the guilt they feel because of their own recent debauched behavior. The Finn, a pathetic character, is left on the dock at Algiers far from home. No ship will take him. His worst fear, to be lost in Africa, is being realized. The Algerian attendant, "his shadow," explains that for the Finn to be lost in the "chaos of Africa" is "le destin." [12]

The potentialities of this sketch are never realized. Appealing as it stands, the sketch is undeveloped; and as such, an impression, it appears substantially unchanged in *The Ocean*.

THE STATE OF VIRGINIA—Venezis tells again, in "The State of Virginia," of the sadness of upheaval, of living in the alien land, of *xeniteia*. An old woman has finally received from her child after thirty years a ticket to America. Originally a refugee from Anatolia, she finds it hard to leave her second home in Attica for a new one in Virginia. Spending the night in vigil with an old friend, she looks "at the peaks of the Attican earth, her second country, now that she must leave for her third country, the final one. Now, she understood that a man can be uprooted only once. Twice is too much; twice is unbearable." [13] Still, the old woman will leave because it is *moira*, "le destin," as is the exile of the Finn in Algiers. These are Venezis' passive characters, sometimes desperate, finally resigned, broken by the winds of chance.

THE HOME OF THE LOST ANGELS—In this narrative Venezis deals with another kind of loss. A mother from the Aegean brings her mentally retarded daughter to Switzerland. Here the child will be placed in the home of Frau Ebberle. Two other girls, a Mongoloid and a paralyzed, brain-damaged child, are in the care of Frau Ebberle, who has no children of her own. The Aegean mother hesitates but leaves her daughter high in the Alps, far from home, knowing she will never see her again. But it must be done, for a normal child at home wishes the death of the defective child and the mother fears for both. The child is left and the narrator remarks:

> For some time after we left, we could hear the painful cries of the child who had been abandoned to its fate. They intermingled with the howls of the other two and with the noise of the car motor. Afterwards, all sounds were lost in the stillness of the mountain.
> Then, the mother began to lament. She said in her grief that only God would not forgive her. But we knew nothing to tell her about God.[14]

In this sketch, which is again a short impression with unfulfilled possibilities, Venezis raises some of the questions he has dealt with earlier in such stories as "Akif" and "Manolis Lekas." The mother's final statement of her guilt in the eyes of God and the narrator's comment imply that God's existence is enigmatic. Otherwise, why does He allow the terrible human suffering that results from the creation of helpless and defective "angels"?

In another sketch, "The Defeated Man and the Raven," the tourist visits the home of Edgar Allan Poe in Fordham. He tells the history of Poe's life as, with Freda, a university student, he looks into the rooms where Poe moved. The caretaker and guide, like all of Venezis' guides, lives in the past. "At times, I think that we are finishing the lives of Edgar and Virginia, who did not have the chance to grow old," she remarks. "We age for them, in their cottage." [15] Poe becomes the symbol of those defeated by the ravens of life; at the same time, he is one who found enough value in life to celebrate in poetry. Their love for Poe's art unifies the tourist, Freda, and the old guide.

In these stories, anecdotes, and accounts, Venezis restates his belief that life defeats men, that war brutalizes them. Too often, joy and youth and love are ever lost and irretrievable. *The De-*

feated abounds in characters who are completely resigned to a spiritually frugal life. Few fight to wrest the fullness of life; instead, they bleakly retreat as they suffer evil and loss.

Structurally, most of the works included here can be called anecdotes rather than short stories. They record in short narrative form interesting incidents. No real plots exist; characters are very generally sketched. The impressionistic method admits enough detail to suggest the theme. If the characters are broadly drawn, they are also by and large passive. While this passive character or victim is found in Venezis' earlier works, there appear, in the stories from the 'twenties to the 'forties, enough active or struggling characters to widen both scope and meaning, and to achieve a more intense emotional effect.

Although the settings are of "the distant world," the themes are familiar. The irony of life among the beloved ruins and tombs of an ancient civilization is a recurring theme. Various aspects of loss are considered. The sadness of exile, loss of homeland, or *xeniteia* is one; loss of joy, youth, love, innocence, certainty or tranquillity is another. Intermingled with these runs the idea that man must submit to his lot in this imperfect world to which good deities, if they exist, are indifferent. One of his critics says, "The characters of Venezis find their ways, find themselves, from the instant they accept their fates, the instant they become conscious of their transience." [16]

Venezis' diction remains constant. Simple, pared to expose the core of feeling, it sings. Nowhere is it false. Even in the shortest anecdotes the language charges the emotional atmosphere. Richly evocative, it sustains the lyrical character present in the earlier works. It intensifies the tonal aura imparted by the themes.

Yet, in both *Wartime* and *The Defeated,* while Venezis touches the truth, he does not reveal it fully. In "The Two Women and The Tower" the reason for the self-imposed exile of the Englishwoman is never made clear; hence, she does not quite ring true. The old woman in "The State of Virginia" is not a living being but a type, as are the guides in "The Night of Asklepios," "Theonichos and Mnisarete," and "The Old Man of the Seine and The Three." The immigrants in "The Immigrant of Grand Canyon" and "The Bandit Pancho Villa" are truer living people, but the first anecdote is too short, and the rambling narrative method of the second diffuse. The Finn in "The Finn of Algiers" is a character with rare possibilities, yet we never come to know him. We know only the narrator's momentary impression, rendered as in a painting—the hopeless man on the dock in Algiers. The same is true of "The Knife of Bataan and The Verses." The boy represents the truth about how war scars youth, but, again, we learn too little. In "The Broken Branch" the boy "with the Aegean eyes" was the truth in wartime Greece, but the story belongs to the sheltered and protected Anna.

Although it gives immediacy, the first person point of view so frequently employed enhances the anecdotal quality of the works. What ought to happen is reported; the reader's emotional response, his empathy, is therefore diminished.

In spite of these flaws Venezis is a good writer by virtue of what he can do when he does it. *The Aegean* and *Winds* are superb works; *Wartime* and *The Defeated* include some fine stories. The short and skillful account "Days of Crete," for example, shows Venezis' reaction to the attack on Crete in 1941 by the German air force and armies. He describes the mood of Greece:

The days of April in 1941 had passed. Full of fire, blood, and steel. And full of barrenness. The men were dead; hope was dead. Greece bent down, exhausted, as if she would stop breathing. The streets of the capital had changed: they were no longer cheerful and bright— the pepper plants, the blue skies. It was a torn Athens, wild and sad. There came down from the north the painful gallery: ragged, bloody, the victors of the mountains of Epirus. But that, too, was ending.[17]

This excellent description expresses well the somber spirit of wartime Greece. Yet war, like everything else in life, passes on. It gives way to time, to what follows. The law of change and renewal applies to authors as well as to history. Venezis continued in the postwar period to work for the Bank of Greece and to write steadily. Some of his postwar writings have already been discussed; however, a whole new category has not. These are books which grew out of his travels abroad and throughout the Greek world.

CHAPTER 6

The Wonders of Travel

I Introduction

THE writing of travelogues, a genre in which Venezis worked after the war, has been popular in many countries including Greece. It reflects a thirst for knowledge on the part of the reader and a thirst for experience, very often, on the part of the author. Several important modern Greek authors besides Venezis, notably Nikos Kazantzakis, have written vivid accounts of their trips abroad. These voyagers are neither Odysseus, Sinbad, nor Marco Polo, but they bring to their discoveries the same sense of wonder. They turn their impressions into literature, and they are read for various reasons: by the young, to learn about other countries and cultures; by the general public, to enjoy the tour vicariously, with a celebrity like Venezis as the guide; and by the scholar, to harvest more intelligence about an author who interests him primarily because he has already won a place in literary history. Some authors visit a country, of course, to ridicule or otherwise condemn its manners and institutions. Many propaganda travelogues of the Cold War assume this political character. But such is not the case with the travel books of Venezis. He does not sully his sense of wonder with polemics nor chill his romantic pleasure with satire.

His first work of this type, *Autumn in Italy* (1950), was intended at first to express the feelings of a Greek visiting in 1948 the country of a people who had been the cruel enemy just a few years before, during the Occupation.[1] Yet the setting in which he composed and the mood it inspired forbade his return to the wartime bitterness. He wrote the book while staying in New York City beside the peaceful Hudson, near Fort Tryon Park and the museum known as the Cloisters, formerly a monastery. At the Cloisters, Venezis paused often to ponder the meaning of two antique statues: one of the crucified Christ and one of the unicorn whose myth, originally from India, had become Christianized. At

the park, with its natural serenity, he pondered other meanings—
of children feeding doves and squirrels, of a mother with her
baby, and of various races (Negro, Chinese, and Caucasian)
bound together by love of grass and trees and sun. Thus he could
not return to the old though justified bitterness in the writing of
Autumn in Italy. "May this chronicle of travel then say only what
it has to say. About the Earth. About Art. About the memory of
Greek Grandeur which once reached to this land of Italy during
the time of Magna Graecia." [2]

In writing about the United States, Venezis has always shown a
warm and uncritical admiration for our history, our democratic
institutions, and our people. He has generously praised the ideals
we profess without seeking to establish how often we profane
them in our practice. We cannot find in Venezis, therefore, the
same subtle sifting of myth from reality that we can in observers
like Lord Bryce and Harold Laski. If the American reader of
America (1955) is not particularly enriched, neither is he annoyed
by the shallow bias and misrepresentation that vitiated many earlier books about us written by European visitors with an aristo-
cratic axe to grind; and he may indeed be reminded, by the
enthusiasm of Venezis, of many forgotten wonders so easily available and so thoroughly unappreciated. Venezis wrote the book, of
course, not for an American but for a Greek audience. In it, one of
their great authors has guided them through a country whose
freedom, power, beauty, and opportunity lured hundreds of thousands of Greek immigrants during the present century.

The writing of *America* grew out of an award granted to Venezis by the United States government under the Smith-Mundt Act,
a law which encouraged foreign intellectuals to visit our country
on an exchange plan and study it at first hand. Venezis, as reported by *Time* on October 24, 1949, was the first writer to receive
the award.[3] For several months, he made the busy and crowded
tour as a guest of the State Department; this became the basis for
his second and most ambitious travelogue. The Greek Hour
broadcast on the Voice of America, on the evening of November
22, 1949, devoted entirely to his life and works, proved one of the
many highlights of his visit to America. The announcer praised
him as a man, as an artist, and as a Greek. He mentioned the fine
reception Venezis received when he described his travel impressions before various groups throughout the nation. "As a Greek,"

the announcer said, "Mr. Venezis was a valuable representative of his country wherever he went, wherever he spoke. Elias Venezis is the first writer from Greece, the first from Europe, the first from the Eastern Hemisphere who has been thus honored—with an invitation from the State Department in line with its program of cultural exchange." [4]

The title of the author's last travelogue, *The Argonauts* (1962), suggests travel on the pattern set by the myth of Jason; however, it is a compilation of several descriptive and narrative articles about different places, properly defined by the sub-title "Chronicles of Greeks and Travels." [5] These articles with their historical and human interest are the kind that Venezis and other famous Greek authors often serialize in the Sunday supplements. They educate and entertain the reader; they add quality and dignity to the journal; and they keep the writer's name before the public, without adding much to his literary reputation. In Greece the writer, especially if he is also an Academician, enjoys a high position as an intellectual with a duty to speak on occasion to the people. The newspaper is his means of contact. Although Venezis has written countless articles and columns for the press, *The Argonauts* comprises not ephermeral pieces but more solid work that deserves the permanence of book publication. Unlike his other travelogues, this book stays within the geographical boundaries of Greece—Corfu, Olympus, Metsovo, Epirus, Lefkas. Its purpose is not to chronicle the personal impressions of Venezis so much as to present aspects of Greek cultural, religious, and literary history. For example, the last article in *The Argonauts* concerns the Ionian island of Lefkas; there the author visits scenes memorialized by famous poets.

II Autumn in Italy

The decision by Venezis not to allow his own feelings as a Greek to color his attitudes toward the former enemy, while writing *Autumn in Italy*, was very wise. It freed his mind to dwell on the deeper spiritual and cultural values of Italian humanism that fascism had debased. The book is divided into five parts: Venice, Florence, Livorno (Leghorn), Rome, and Magna Graecia. In recording each of his visits Venezis combines key aspects of the past and present of the place in order to bring out its essence. Wherever he goes he is alert to historical relationships between Greece and Italy going back to the classical age.

The section on Venice begins with an episode from the Renaissance, at the end of the fifteenth century during the height of Venetian power, when a Greek pirate caught in the Aegean is brought in chains to the Doge's palace. All about him is the splendor of Venice, the "Queen of the Seas." The Venetians wish to enlist the strong surly Greek into their service against the Turks. They try to impress him; they take him before the Great Council; they show him the art of Venice. For his adamant "No" the Venetians execute him with the blow of an axe.

Venezis tours the city looking for remaining signs of the power that made Venice the mistress of the seas and, through conquest, had set fire to the Greek islands. As he goes along the Grand Canal the legend of Venice awakens for him. Now and then the gondolier cries out the name of a tourist attraction. "The Ducal Palace!" From this great white building, now dormant, flowed the power that for three centuries dominated the Aegean. Venezis gets off near the Bridge of Sighs because he wants to explore the luxurious quarters of the Doge of Venice.

The time is November, a crisp cool morning. Between the Italian Alps and the Adriatic, as the author ponders the past, lies the Doge's Palace which he now enters, to find the peculiar solitude that attends all places of departed glory. Inside, he pauses at the Room of Arms where he finds a gallery of Venetian heroes that includes Greeks: a statue of Francisco Mavrogeno, a Peloponnesian; and of Ugo Foscolo, a fierce sea captain of Greek descent. In another room the sun enters to brighten paintings by Tintoretto, Titian, and Veronese. Venezis writes, "So much glory, so much blood, so much pain, so many tears, was it only for this?" [6]

At the great cathedral of St. Marks, Venezis notices the four golden horses above the main entrance. The statues were appropriated from Byzantium in the year 1204. Venezis develops the analogy of Greece as a Tree of Lights whose roots can never be destroyed. The more that barbarians have invaded and hurt Greece, the more her light has spread. Before the four horses, another evidence of Greek light, passed the entire glory of Venice. The author feels strongly nationalistic as he thinks of the Greek miracle, the spreading of Greek light. Not distant from the tombs of the Doges he comes upon "The Bridge of the Greeks" and an old Hellenic Orthodox Church, Saint George. There he meets an elderly candle lighter, originally from the island of Serifos.

In the city of Florence, Venezis visits the monastic cell of Heironymus Savonarola. This legendary figure of the Renaissance intrigues him. To understand those who burned people at the stake, and were themselves burned, Venezis writes, one must see Florence for the first time at night, to get lost in the streets near the Arno, in the bitter cold, soon after the end of a great war. He describes Savonarola as a ferocious enemy of beauty, of love, of women, of the painting of women, of learning, and of joy—in short, of all that inspired Lorenzo the Magnificent, his chief rival for power. Later, Venezis searches for traces of Savonarola in the Vatican library; there he sees the autograph of this "demon of the Renaissance" and notes a paradox: the demon wrote with a delicate girlish hand!

Also in Florence, Venezis seeks traces left by Dante and by Michelangelo. He notes the former's birthplace, the street named Via Alighieri, and a statue in the Palazzo Vecchio. The Greek writer wonders which Dante is thus honored, the great poet or the politician whom Florence forced into exile. The answer is Dante the poet, returned in fame as the saint of letters. "He became a legendary glory of the world," Venezis writes (p. 52). He walks up the same road to the hermitage of San Salvatore of the Mountain that Michelangelo also loved. Venezis recalls the genius of the master, his obsession with faces and bodies, his immortal work in the Sistine Chapel, his *David*. Upon his descent from "the chapel of Michelangelo," Venezis unexpectedly meets a man alone, a victim of the recent war, whom he calls the madman of Florence. The man searches among the ruins for something he loved and lost.

Livorno is the next Italian city that Venezis visits. Here at the port where merchant vessels put in to load coal (as described in his novel *The Ocean*), Venezis sees extensive war ruins and a girl with a white bird in a cage. She has trained the bird to pick up fortune cards; the one she gives to Venezis tells of his happiness. He meets a fellow Greek who had dreamed of America but had never managed to go there. He then has the interesting adventure of riding a lift to the top of a neighboring mountain, Montenero.

In a quaint church reminiscent of the Renaissance, he says a prayer for the little girl with the bird and the cage.

In Rome he gathers impressions not only of the city itself but also of the Appian Way, the Vatican, the graves of Shelley and Keats, and the Villa Borghese, a museum. In the city he visits various places of interest: the Colosseum, the Capital, and St. Peter's Square where he finds two Greek statues near that of Marcus Aurelius. On the square during the Second World War the Germans stacked their arms and, confronted by the Swiss Guards of the Vatican, they fled. At St. Peter's, Venezis inspects the immortal art treasures of the Vatican including the *Pieta* of Michelangelo and his ceiling in the Sistine Chapel. Of much interest to him is the castle of San Angelo to which the Popes traditionally retired in moments of personal danger.

Together with two women, one French and the other Greek, Venezis pays homage at the gravesites of Shelley and Keats. The Frenchwoman comes each year to worship the art of Rome. Venezis learns that Shelley's grave is always provided with fresh flowers by admirers, and that not all of him is buried here. The Frenchwoman tells how Shelley's heart was saved from the crematory flames by Byron and Trelawny for burial in England. The Greek tourist reads on the gravestone these lines from Shakespeare's *The Tempest:*

> Nothing of him that doth fade,
> But doth suffer a sea-change
> Into something rich and strange.
> (p. 96)

Venezis recalls the famous remark by Shelley to the effect that "We are all Greeks." Our laws, our literature, our religion, our art —all have their roots in Greece (p. 91). At the grave of Keats he reads the touching epitaph: "This grave contains all that was mortal of a young English poet who, on his death bed, in the bitterness of his heart at the malicious power of his enemies, desired these words to be engraved on his tombstone: 'Here lies one whose name was writ in water'" (p. 17). The visitors from afar, including Venezis, stay too long into the twilight. They are almost locked inside the cemetery.

At the Villa Borghese, in the art museum, Venezis the next morning is moved by a sudden reminder of Greece: two paintings by El Greco. They are *The Baptism of Christ* and *The Birth of Christ*. Near the paintings of the master born in Crete are the works of other Renaissance masters, such as Raphael and Tintoretto. With a nationalistic feeling Venezis comments, "Here then, even here, in a small room in the Villa Borghese, is our fatherland" (p. 103).

In an episode at the zoo, the author refers to a Greek writer (actually himself) who told a story about a camel with a white head. It was one of the travelers' tales in *Beyond the Aegean*. Venezis states the author was certain that such an unusual camel was impossible to find. And yet, here in the zoo at Rome, as he writes, "It was in truth the camel of the story told in that book, it was the camel with the white head!" (p. 105). In an iron enclosure, the camel plays like a deer, unaware of the mysterious need of its seekers that it be truly lost forever.

In the final section of the book, Magna Graecia, Venezis describes his stay in southern Italy. On the train to Naples he sees Mount Vesuvius, the famous volcano. In the city there are still wartime ruins. The statue of Dante that stands in Naples is more in the warmer southern mood; the poet is alive, more ready to argue, to create havoc. In the twilight, overlooking the beautiful bay, Venezis thinks again about the past. The enlightening power of Greater Greece had once reached these shores.

He pursues the theme of Greek influence when he goes to the Land of the Greeks, that region of slopes and terraces which is composed of the lava of Mount Vesuvius. People still live, he finds, up near the crater, near the "lips of death." Many of them are craftsmen who make artifacts of coral for sale to tourists as souvenirs. At the quiet dead city of Pompeii, Venezis pauses for a moment to hear, in his mind, the tragic sounds of the catastrophe of 79 A.D. The land of lava stirs again with ghosts of ancient Greeks; then the sight of a living dog returns the author to the present.

The travelogue ends with a boat trip to Sorrento, Capri, and the villa of St. Michael, made memorable for Venezis in a book by the Swedish writer Axel Munthe. Years before, the Swede had come to the cliffs of Capri seeking the traces of the Roman tyrant Tiberius. Fate had brought Tiberius here in self-imposed exile; fate, or "the spirit of the place," also brought Axel Munthe who paid for the serenity he found by losing his sight. Venezis inspects Tiberius' palace and the grotto where, according to Tacitus, the tyrant strangled children. Venezis recounts Munthe's successful battle to save from slaughter the migratory birds that habitually rested on Capri. The mountain top apparently belonged to a dealer in live birds who trapped them by the thousands and sold them to hostelries throughout Europe. Axel Munthe, a doctor, miraculously saved the butcher's life, and in return was promised that the birds would never again be molested. At twilight, with the sun going down, the trip to St. Michael ends.

In the brief epilogue Venezis informs us that he took the plane from Rome for the return to Greece. He thinks of the living dog among the ruins of Pompeii and of the new lava that man has brought upon himself, the lava of war.

III America

The travelogue on the United States, much longer than the earlier one on Italy, employs the same general style and technique. Venezis writes simply and concretely, in usually short and uncomplicated sentences. He breaks up the descriptive pattern by frequent snatches of dialogue with people he meets, and by dramatizing brief episodes from the trip itself or from recollected history. Whenever the locale permits, he likes to evoke its mood and to make it sentient with a kind of mystical meaning. Such a practice, of course, can be overdone, in which case the result is obscurantism, sentimentalism, and pathetic fallacy. Venezis manages to avoid these pitfalls.

America, the travel book that was actually sponsored by the State Department, retraces a happy journey that begins in Salem, Massachusetts, crosses the country by a northern route, and returns *via* the South to end in Washington, D.C. Much of the text is based, or could be based, on the booklets available at most tourist attractions. The rest of the material reflects the author's immediate experience as well as his previously acquired knowledge of America. For the reader in Greece, especially the youth, the book is an excellent albeit uncritical look at the United States. For Americans, it can serve as a reminder of certain sacred aspects of our heritage. The book also helps us to discover the attitudes of Venezis himself.

He begins in Salem where the Puritans once hanged people for witchcraft. He visits the house in which they were condemned. The replica of the *Arabella,* John Winthrop's ship, makes him dwell on the courage of the colonists in crossing the ocean on such a flimsy craft. Venezis recalls with animation the legendary voyage of the *Mayflower,* the hardships of the first years, the religious difficulties of Roger Williams, the origin of Thanksgiving, the witch trials and how they began. With respect to the trials Venezis comments, "Europe had sent to New England, as shown by events, her wild, her fanatic, spirit." [7] An author himself, he is moved by the birthplace of Nathaniel Hawthorne. He is also impressed by the actual house of the seven gables immortalized in Hawthorne's novel. He describes the "large old wooden house, black with time," which he regards as symbolic of the entire New England past (p. 21). Inside he goes from room to room where he sees many Hawthorne mementoes.

Venezis divides his chapter on Boston between the old city and the new. The Common, Beacon Hill, the Charles River, the *Atlantic Monthly,* Louisburg Square—these familiar landmarks he notes, as well as the Yankee's allegedly flinty heart based on love of money. The quietness of Louisburg Square will be broken by choristers on Christmas Eve. Turning to the past, he recalls the Boston Massacre (March 5, 1770), the Tea Party (December 17, 1773), and briefly traces the start of the American Revolution. In the rain he goes to the Old Granary Burial Ground where he reads the epitaph written by Franklin at the grave of his parents. He concludes his impressions of Boston at King's Chapel and its quaint little cemetery.

At Concord, that rich repository of Americana, Venezis crosses the bridge where, as Emerson wrote, the shot heard around the world was fired on April 19, 1775. He compares the three-hundred-year heritage of Concord with the three-thousand-year heritage of Greece. He mentions Emerson, Alcott, and Hawthorne. Near the statue of the Minute Man he reads the touching inscription on the graves of the English soldiers; in part it states: "They came three thousand miles and died to keep the past upon its throne" (p. 35). Venezis briefly lingers at the Old Manse. Night has fallen.

Before leaving for Niagara Falls, he visits Cambridge where he tours Harvard and the home of Longfellow. He sketches the history of the university and its present scope of learning, the various schools, Widener Library, the house system, the *Lampoon*. At the Fogg Museum of Art he marvels at the famed glass flowers; and at the International Student Center he meets students with various backgrounds, but finds the Greek girl among them the prettiest of all! When asked why he wants to see Longfellow's house since the poetry is in his books, Venezis answers, "I love Longfellow. The poetry is not only the books. Poetry is also the man. I want to find the traces of the man. I want to live those traces" (p. 41). His enthusiasm for Longfellow surpasses any feeling he has for the Concord immortals. What he likes about the leading New England poet is his "exaltation" and his poetic use of myth. "The myth of Europe, the myth of Greece" (p. 41).

Venezis leaves places in the East renowned for intellectual power to discover, on his way West, places renowned for natural and industrial power: Niagara Falls and Detroit. He finds the falls exceedingly impressive, describing them eloquently. Again and again he repeats, "The roar! The roar!" To get as close as he can to the elemental force, he rides on the "Maid of the Mist" to the edge of the cataract. He calls the experience "wild and fine." At the Niagara museum he sees an exhibit of Egyptian mummies, among them that of a princess, sister of King Amenhotep III. Did her astrologer foresee, he asks, that her final resting place would be across the seas in America, at Niagara?

At the Ford plant in Dearborn, Venezis hopes to observe what the machine is doing to man. What he finds there is to him a prime example of rugged individualism in its purest and most romantic form. Even college students who are rich men's sons get summer jobs at Ford, because they are determined to make their own way. The idyll of American industrialism is concretely confirmed for him when he see 26,000 cars, owned by Ford employees, in the parking lot. The celebrated assembly line from steel mill to finished product moves Venezis enormously. It symbolizes the power of man. The workers are cheerful and satisfied. He also praises Greenfield Village which Ford established as an authentic replica of the past. He exclaims, "How fine it all was!" (p. 70).

In Chicago, Venezis finds quiet along Lake Michigan at the Adler Planetarium to which he goes after touring the Art Institute. A banker himself, he describes the activity at the Board of Trade as "pandemonium" and "nightmare." The city of the *Tribune,* the stockyards, and Hull House affords Venezis the chance to meet fellow Greeks at the Greek Village restaurant on Halsted near Polk. Chicago also offers him the greatest spectacle of his entire tour: the Music Festival at Soldier Field where a hundred thousand people gather to applaud the songs and dances presented by the city's ethnic groups. One of the three judges for the contest is Venezis' own sister-in-law, the singer Elena Nicolaidi.

Hull House and the Greek Village inspire ten of the most deeply felt pages in *America*. They concern the Greek immigrants, their reasons for leaving home, their trials and progress in the New World. Into the unknown they voyaged seeking the myth of riches, leaving behind their loved ones, and giving substance to many a sad poem and song. "Have you seen my boy, my *pallikari?*" (p. 79). Pride often kept them here, Venezis writes, and not the great success they pretended to be. In letters home they never spoke of their troubles; they sent back photos of themselves in elegant dress, even though they slaved hard and long, ate badly, and slept together a dozen in a room. And yet they slowly rooted themselves in the Land of Opportunity, raised families, and maintained their identity within the greater society.

From Chicago and the grandeur of people Venezis entrains for Colorado and the grandeur of the mountains. Like most Greeks, he venerates mountains because they symbolize the struggle for freedom. Also, they are the traditional home of the gods. For Venezis they recall the magical youth he narrates in *Beyond the Aegean*. Needless to say, the Rocky Mountains fulfill all his expectations. Natural attractions that excite him are Mount Evans, Echo Lake, Idaho Springs, the Red Rocks, the Garden of the Gods, Williams Canyon, the Cave of the Winds, and Pike's Peak. To get there he had passed through the green prairie and the dry brown pastures. How many immigrant laborers, among them Greeks, had laid the tracks over which his train rumbled?

On the night train to the country of the Mormons, Venezis ponders the European's misconception of the United States. Everything here is supposedly big city, skyscraper, the rush to get rich. "The real face of America," he writes, "is the endless land, fields and forests, the green tilled land—the blessing of God" (p. 110). America is mainly a nation of small towns filled with small wooden houses. After these ruminations he records his visit to Salt Lake City. He retells the history of Joseph Smith and

his Mormons. He visits the famous Tabernacle, tastes the water of
Salt Lake, and watches the gulls, the state bird of Utah and the
sacred bird of the Mormons.

Venezis journeys on the Western Pacific past the wastelands of
Nevada, heading for California. "How distant from New York!"
he exclaims. "How distant from Greece!" (p. 121). He watches
the sun set behind the Golden Gate Bridge. At Stanford University
the Greek novelist attends the installation of a new chancellor.
After he examines the Spreckels Museum, Venezis goes to a San
Francisco beach. Alone with the gulls, he thinks of the early con-
quistadors, and of one named Juan de Fouca alleged to be a
Greek.

Before going to Hollywood, the indispensable attraction, Venezis pays a visit to the "kingdom of the sequoias" and the Yosemite
where he is awed by the giant redwoods. The American system of
National Parks is of great interest to him because for many years he
proposed similar parks for Greece. He says that their establishment might have once been an aspect of romanticism, but that is
no longer the case. He quotes Sigurd Olson, an official of the
Parks, to this effect: "Wild and virginal nature is a spiritual need
of the American people. It is the antidote to the great pressure
which modern life forces upon us, a means for man to find peace
and equilibrium. Wild and virginal nature is a need of the soul"
(p. 144).

Venezis contrasts Los Angeles and Hollywood to this unspoiled
aspect of the West Coast. "What a city!" he repeats about the "city
of angels." He notes its Spanish past, its many Spanish influences,
and its current hurry and sprawl. His quick tour of Hollywood
includes Grauman's Chinese Theater where stars write their
names in concrete, and the studios of Metro-Goldwyn-Mayer,
where he witnesses the shooting of a scene from the Civil War
film *The Outriders*. From what he sees at MGM he notes the various steps in producing a movie: the writing, the directing, the
shooting. It is very late that evening when he gets back to Los
Angeles, a smoggy city at night.

On his return east Venezis takes the southerly route through
Arizona, New Mexico, New Orleans, then over to Florida and up
to New York and Washington. In Arizona, he learns, the typical
holding is a ranch busy with cowboys, many of them Mexicans,
taking care of vast herds of cattle. On the ranch he sees and de-

scribes the cutting of horns on steers; it is a bloody business, the
creatures moaning in pain. Both in Arizona and in New Mexico
the Greek traveler experiences the only authentic Americans left,
the Indians. At the Papago Indian Reservation he finds that the
remnants of the tribe are mostly Christians who had forgotten
their old gods. He asks three aged Indian women if they had ever
left the reservation; one answers that she had been to California.
She returned because "The voice of the desert is strong" (p. 179).
When asked what happened to their feathers, she replies, "The
white man came and took away the feathers" (p. 179). On another occasion, at the bottom of the Grand Canyon, Venezis
watches some tribal dances of the Hopi Indians. And in New Mexico, which he calls the land of enchantment, he observes the pueb-
los and the cliff dwellers where once a community prospered despite the surrounding wasteland.

At Tucson Venezis has a literary discussion with Erskine Caldwell. The American novelist states his view that literature here
does not express ethnic character in the same way that it does in
Europe. America is too broad, too various; its writing expresses
the national through the locality and the region. As for its gloom
and pessimism, Caldwell says that most American writers derive
from the lower classes and write about the life they know best. Of
great interest to the guest from Greece is Caldwell's library. It is
crowded, among much else, with first editions of his works, with
photographs, and with literary awards. Altogether it is a pleasant
encounter for Venezis.

Flying east to New Orleans, he gets his first glimpse of the Mississippi river from the air. Venezis relates the story of LaSalle and
facts about the river, the Louisiana Purchase, and Old Orleans
which was a haven for pirates like Lafitte. In the old quarter he
suddenly sees an astonishing sign: "Greek Club Acropolis." It
helps to confirm what he already knows, that Greeks live all over
America. After touring the city, he crosses the Mississippi by
bridge to get a last look at its grandeur. He finds himself in a
Negro section whose poverty, stagnation, and filth appall him.
"The women fat, black as tar, wild" (p. 224). Venezis is uneasy
with Negroes. They seem to frighten him.

At his next pause, Tarpon Springs, he meets the famous Greek
sponge divers. He attends their church, St. Nicholas, whose priest
yearly blesses the waters and the sponge boats that provide a pre-

carious living for the swarthy immigrants from the Aegean Islands. Venezis browses about the waterfront, talks with various people, and gazes off at the sea. He listens to the account of Johnny Gonatas who had made a film called *The Story of the Sponge* on which he realized $50,000 from tourists who paid a few cents each to see it. Gonatas tells him the *National Geographic Magazine* had featured him in a display about the sponge divers. He also tells of making a movie with Elia Kazan, the great director.

Venezis concludes his American journey with stops in New York and Washington. He is fascinated by the surge and color of Times Square, the quaintness of Greenwich Village, the subway, Broadway's blaze of neon, Radio City, the Empire State Building. He rides to Hyde Park to pay his homage to the memory of Franklin D. Roosevelt. He visits the gravesite as well as the room where FDR was born. Back in the city, Venezis enjoys one of the highlights of his American sojourn: a broadcast by the N.B.C. Orchestra conducted by Dmitri Mitropoulos. Also featured on the program is Elena Nicolaidi. Commenting on the Mitropoulos style, he says, "It is something very strong and very Greek" (p. 258). A long talk with the conductor brings out the interesting admission by Mitropoulos that by memorizing the score he can turn matter into spirit, and thus gain power.

In Washington, D.C., Venezis evidences deep admiration for our democratic heritage. Washington today, he says, is the heart of the world. His view of our capital is thoroughly idealistic and romantic as has been, in the main, his view of America as a whole. Through this rosy perspective he visits all the familiar places: Arlington National Cemetery, Mount Vernon, the Library of Congress, the Lincoln Memorial, the White House, the Ford Theater, and so on. The city is green and beautiful; the people he meets are courteous and warm. In the city's architecture he notices the Greek classical influence everywhere. Venezis states again the unity in diversity which composes America's population. It is a unity structured not only on ethnic and racial groups but also on regionalisms that are harmonious within themselves. It is such a system, still animated by the principles of Abraham Lincoln, that gives new life and power to the Greek ideal of democracy. At the National Gallery he sees the *Laocoön* by El Greco; at the Friar Gallery he finds Alexander the Great in a Persian manuscript.

Venezis concludes the report on his American visit with these words: "Alexander the Great, the Persian manuscript, El Greco, the *Laocoön*, and the green city of a distant people" (p. 274).

IV   The Argonauts

The first of the several chronicles in this travelogue concerns Cyprus. Entitled "The Cave," it recounts the author's going to the island after the Cypriote struggle against the British. He inspects a number of old chapels and monasteries whose construction, religious art, and manuscripts are discussed in relation to the island's history. Venezis devotes most of his sketch to the cave, now a patriotic shrine, where the British had killed a youthful leader of EOKA, the underground army. Cyprus, the legendary land of copper, has again been a land of blood, courage, and honor. Fading on walls are the slogans of the recent battle, such as "Freedom for Cyprus." Venezis quotes from the poet Kostis Palamas to the effect that the greatness of a nation is measured not only in *stremmata* (a portion of land) but also in blood.[8]

The main interest in "The Cave" is the life and death of the Cypriote hero, Gregory Avxentios. At the monastery of Mahaira, Venezis goes through the museum which contains the hero's watch, his knife, his clothes, his grenade, and even the rock on which he died. All are blackened by the flaming gasoline that killed him. Born in 1928, he grew up brave and strong; he worked in the fields but also loved history and literature. In his later teens he went to Greece for higher schooling but could not overcome the deficiencies in his preparation. Back on Cyprus, Gregory underwent three years of military service and soon after, in 1955, the church bells started ringing for freedom and union with Greece. The struggle was on, and Gregory found himself a guerilla leader of EOKA. Near the monastery, in a cave, he had his headquarters; but a muleteer informed on him. The British arrived with guns, tear gas, and smoke bombs, and with gasoline which they spilled into the cave and ignited. Venezis examines the charred cave. He reads the funeral song composed for the son by the grieving mother—as is customary for mothers to do in Cyprus.

In the "Journey to Olympus" the author is invited by the famous mountain climber Francis Farquhar to accompany his party to the summit of Greece's mythical home of the gods. In the group is the "conqueror of Mount Olympus," Christos Kakalos. Now an old man but still hardy, he reached the top of Mitika, the loftiest peak, on August 2, 1913. Also in the group are Farquhar's wife, Marjorie, and a Greek woman companion. Venezis mentions *La Grèce Immortelle,* which tells of the exploits of Kakalos, and *Mount Olympus,* written by Farquhar after he climbed in 1914 to a peak that missed being the highest by twelve meters. "The beauty of Olympus," Venezis quotes from *La Grèce Immortelle,* "is a spiritual beauty" (p. 48). The need to climb it to the top is a spiritual need.

On a sunny day in June the little caravan begins the ascent. Venezis misses neither the physical grandeur nor the symbolism of the famous mountain. The deep woods are easily peopled with dragons. The climbers pass the ruins of a Byzantine monastery which the Turks first destroyed in 1828, during the Greek Revolution, and which the Germans destroyed again during the Occupation—and for the same reason, because the monks helped the fighters for freedom. They spend the night near the ruins. The next day the weather worsens; black rain clouds form about the peaks before them. Thunder, the speech of the gods, rumbles in the heavens. In sight of the summit Venezis speaks with Farquhar who quietly weeps for a son who recently died. He has come to Mount Olympus, Farquhar says, in order to understand man. For his part Venezis has brought along the *Iliad.* "Olympus thus, at the hour when all about us the shadows were falling, became again identical with Homer, became spiritual eternity" (p. 65).

Farquhar's caravan must reach the top of Mitika by ten o'clock of the third morning; otherwise the clouds will blanket the view. It is from there, from Mitika, that Greece begins all her legends. Great fog banks creep down upon the climbers, the progress grows more difficult. The old man of Olympus, Kakalos, forges ahead while the rest follow. Then he turns and welcomes them. They have arrived! Tired, they sit and marvel at their exploit. Venezis opens his *Iliad.* Farquhar says, "One purpose of life has concluded" (p. 72). Everything is now in bright light. A thousand meters below are the clouds, white and thick, like another ocean.

The longest of the four divisions of the book, on Epirus, is called "In the Land of Prophets and Oracles." Venezis journeys to Metsovo in the heart of the rugged Pindus Mountains; he not only describes the town but also speaks about gods and brigands, about Turks, Italians, and Romans who figure in the "Chronicle of

Epirus." Certain civil and religious freedoms granted to Metsovo
by the Sultan's Grand Vizier in 1655 helped to make it an outstanding Greek center of commerce and culture within the Otto-
man Empire. Venezis contrasts its gods with those of Olympus.
The Olympian gods are more like human beings. They bicker
among themselves, they make love, they deceive, they play with
fortune. The gods of Metsovo, being Christian, give their dark
divination and "leave man to make out alone, without any help,
struggling with himself and with heaven, with his soul and with
death" (p. 75). The land, too, in keeping with this spiritual auster-
ity, is hard, frugal, bare.

In the fine narrative, "The Wolves," Venezis writes about a
young newly married couple sent to one of the remotest of Epirotic towns, Souli, to conduct a school for the children of isolated
shepherds high in the mountains. Actually, the school is located
on the ruins of Souli, destroyed by the Albanians of Ali Pashi during the Greek revolution. Up the only and perilous path the
teacher and his bride hike, led by Thanasis Tokas, a shepherd of
Samoniva. During the arduous climb Tokas talks about the regional myths and legends. They spend the night in Samoniva. The
next day, when the newcomers reach their destination, they are
bitterly disappointed. There is no town, only the school. But they
say to each other, "We will get used to it." Tokas insists the people
will help them with food and wood for the winter.

The neighboring shepherd families pay them a call on Sunday,
with their priest. The simple superstitious women tell them not to
search the ruins for a golden cradle, or the huge snake that guards
it will strike them. Also, they must fear the wolves that will stalk
their hut in the cold of winter. Months pass, the teacher works and
reads; but the wife, who is now pregnant, gets more and more
hysterical about the wolves. She dreads a stillbirth induced by her
own panic. More and more she equates the wolves with the possible death of her child.

One night, in the bitter lonely winter, she looks out and thinks
she sees a wolf near the school. Her husband at her side glimpses
only a shadow. She determines to leave the very next day, to return home to Corfu despite her advanced pregnancy. The wolf,
her husband says, is a test of their love. She leaves anyway. He
remains alone. He wants to see if the wolf really exists, that his
life be not destroyed merely by the shadow of a fear. "But it

seems that the work of wolves," Venezis writes, "is not to help man" (p. 135). The wolf never reappears.

In the section entitled "Legends of Epirus" Venezis deals with the past and present of the fabled city of Yannina. Like Metsovo, Yannina was also a Greek center and refuge while Athens was still a Turkish town. Not only were the Greeks numerous in Yannina, but so were the Jews. They used the Jewish alphabet, Venezis avers, to write the Greek language. They patterned their songs on Greek folk songs. Their ancestors, of course, had settled in Yannina after having been driven out of Spain by the Inquisition.

One of the Epirotic legends concerns the two abortive revolts against the Turks led by Bishop Dionysios. The first, in Thessaly, occurred in 1600 and was drowned in blood. The bishop escaped but another cleric, Serafim, was skewered alive. Later the church declared him a saint. The second revolt took place in Epirus in 1611 when Bishop Dionysios was seventy. Like the first it also ended in a disastrous slaughter of the Christians. The Turks captured Dionysios, skinned him alive, and filled his skin with straw. Not only did they exhibit the ghastly thing in towns throughout Epirus; they also took it to Constantinople to show the Sultan.

Another legend deals with the greatest *pallikari* of Epirus, Katsandonis, and the notorious Ali Pasha who killed him. The time is shortly before the Greek Revolution of 1821. Captured through betrayal, the freedom fighter Katsandonis is brought before Ali Pasha in Yannina. Ali orders his executioners to rip the flesh from his bones little by little to prolong the hero's agony. Throughout the night Katsandonis lives in absolute pain. When he dies, Venezis writes, the Jews secretly gather the dismembered body and sell it to the elders of the place, to the Christians, for proper burial. The Greeks won revenge for their martyred hero when they killed Ali Pasha on January 17, 1822. His body with severed head was brought to Yannina.

Venezis moves the chronicles of Epirus forward to modern times. He writes of the heroic poet Lorenzo Mavilis, a lover of freedom like Thomas Paine, who fought against the Turks in the Cretan Revolution of 1896 and again in the Graeco-Turkish War of 1897. He was killed at the Battle of Driscou in the Balkan War of 1912. Venezis also writes of the Italian general Rizziotti Garibaldi, of the famed patriotic family, who in 1912 arrived to fight the Turks with his own battalion. Finally, to conclude the report of

his travels in Epirus, Venezis writes "A Greek Lady and a Dane."
The lady, Angelica Hatzimichael, was well-known for her pioneer-
ing work in promoting the folk arts and crafts of her region. The
Dane, Carsten Höeg, had composed a two-volume study of the
Sarakatsan folk of the Pindus Mountains, among whom he lived.
He dealt with their history, their culture, and their language.
Höeg's last visit to Greece was in 1957, shortly before his death,
when he went to Patmos to photograph old musical manuscripts.
Höeg, the friend of Venezis, typifies the European whose love for
Greece follows closely upon his knowledge of her.

The last of the four major sections of *The Argonauts,* called
"The Eternal Glory," is based on the author's going to the fabled
island of poets, Lefkas, and to the equally renowned Delphi
where the oracle of Apollo once helped rule the destinies of man.
On Lefkas, the Ionian isle much punished by earthquakes, Venezis enters the house and the room where the great modern demotic poet, Anghelos Sikelianos, was born. The women of Lefkas,
he notes, are proud and tall; they get their splendid posture in
part from carrying jugs of water and other objects on their heads.
He is invited to a feast honoring a very old lady; she is photographed surrounded by all her kin that she may be remembered
after she dies.

At the tiny island of Madouri, lying between Lefkas and Akar-
nania, Venezis walks among the memories of the first major poet
to champion demotic Greek, Aristoteles Valaorites. He did so
from the 1880's on. Venezis pauses in the shade of the huge pines
which the poet set out himself. Back on Lefkas, he visits the grave
of a German professor, Wilhelm Doerpfeld, who had been with
Schliemann at the excavations for Troy. At an ecstatic moment
Doerpfeld had once told Venezis that in his opinion Ithaca, the
mythical kingdom of Odysseus, was the modern Lefkas!

At the cemetery at Delphi, Venezis finds the grave of Harikleia
Sikelianos, mother of the poet. The famous son composed the epitaph for her stone. High above the town of Delphi, on a cliff,
stands the house where Anghelos Sikelianos and his wife, Eva,
lived during most of the days of his fame. The house is practically
in ruins. During the war many a battle was fought in its vicinity.
In it lives a family that has migrated to the mainland of Greece
from the Dodecanese Islands, together with a student and several
others. Venezis looks over several bits of manuscript which are

clearly those of the poet. He writes, "We left Delphi with a tightening of the heart. But we did not know that Delphi was preparing something else at the homesite of Sikelianos" (p. 228).

That something else allows Venezis to conclude his Grecian travelogue on a tragic note in keeping with his constant emphasis on the blindness and irony of fate. A short while later, in Athens, he is visited by the student he had met in Delphi. As he left the Sikelianos house, the student said, he saw the two older boys of the Dodecanese family, aged eight and six, playing together in the nearby sand. He had hardly reached the main road leading down to Delphi, however, when he heard a loud explosion at the house. The children had exploded a forgotten land mine. Not only had it killed them; it had scattered them into little pieces. Venezis stresses the irony embodied in the horror: that it should happen here, at the house of Anghelos Sikelianos, where had lived so much poetry, so much beauty, so much love, so much passion.

Venezis has written other travel accounts besides those in *Autumn in Italy, America,* and *The Argonauts.* These reports have usually taken the form of articles in Greek newspapers. They may add something to his fame as a journalist, as a man of letters, but little or nothing to his stature as an artist. In his travel books, as discussed above, he indicates minor interest in the basic politics, economics, or current social problems of the countries he tours. He hardly ever allows anything of a genuinely controversial nature to enter into his thinking; if it does in fact, he takes great care not to embarrass by criticism or humor those who have been his hosts in a strange land. What he does indicate is a lively interest in natural grandeur, historical background, cultural achievements, monuments to human greatness, and the people themselves.

CHAPTER 7

The Man of Letters

I The 1950's and Later

THE election of Elias Venezis to the Athens Academy in 1957
capped a literary career crowded with achievement and
recognition both in Greece and abroad. As he states in an article,
he was the first of the Asia Minor writers to receive such recognition.[1] The coveted honor coincided with his retirement from the
Bank of Greece and his assumption soon after of new duties as
director of the National Theater. By this time Venezis had become
a man of letters in every sense of the word; indeed, the 1950's
were an unusually prolific decade for him. Besides many
newspaper and magazine articles, he wrote and published seven
books. Among them are two histories, *Archbishop Damaskinos*
and *Chronicle of the Bank of Greece*, and another novel, *The
Ocean*. Unfortunately, these volumes add very little to the author's literary reputation. If that reputation grew, it did so mainly
because of newer editions of his old masterpieces and further
translations of them abroad. The creative power which Venezis
had shown earlier seemed to get siphoned off into works of lesser
aesthetic quality.

As a man of letters, then, his interest has been to produce whatever presented itself to him fairly readily instead of undergoing
those agonizing reappraisals needed to develop and deepen his
art. The young scholars and writers of Greece, the keepers of aesthetic faith, respect Venezis for what he has done, but they expect
little more from him either in terms of high achievement or of
insight to nourish their own hunger for critical understanding. He
has been, they say, too much the conformist, too much the banker,
too much the Academician, too much a member of the Establishment, in a nation rife with social, literary, and political issues
upon which he has been reluctant to pronounce. That he chooses
to be non-controversial is, of course, his own business. The reasons
that his art has not shown a pattern of growth, however, will come

under ever closer scrutiny by the historians of Greek Literature. One very likely cause may be his inability or unwillingness to probe more deeply, through action, character, and idea, the profoundly tortured soul of postwar Greece.

As a man of letters and journalist, Venezis has composed for the ephemeral press, for Greek journals, hundreds of articles on a wide variety of subjects. In this capacity he employs an easy, simple, and flexible style of language that flows naturally from the equally relaxed demotic of his fiction. The popular magazine *Nea Estia* has been one of the frequent outlets for his better journalistic pieces. *Nea Estia* has also published excerpts of both prose and fiction from his books. In addition, Venezis has written a regular column for the Athens newspaper *Acropolis* under the heading: "Life and Thought, the Chronicle of Academician Elias Venezis." Quite frequently, too, the Greek-American press serializes and otherwise reprints articles and stories by Venezis for its limited audience.

Of more consequence than his ephemeral writings are the three books from his later period mentioned above. The first of these, *Archbishop Damaskinos* (1952), records the activities of the Archbishop of Athens during the years of the German Occupation.[2] Most of the extensive text consists of reproduced letters and other official documents held together by brief editorial comments from the author. He has presented these documents more as primary sources than as material thoroughly digested and integrated with a theory or a thesis about the archbishop, his church, and his politics. The overall effect, if the monotony of the reading can be discounted, is to eulogize rather than to evaluate. After the liberation, Archbishop Damaskinos headed an interim Greek government charged with the duty of liquidating the tragic civil war and restoring political order. In his chronicle Venezis stops short of the events in which Archbishop Damaskinos played a controversial political role, favoring a rightist and royalist restoration. Venezis must have had his reasons for failing to deal with this most dramatic and historic period of the archbishop's noteworthy life. It may well be that the political situation in Greece, as of 1952, was still too sensitive for a genuinely objective interpretation of those events, a bitter civil war, that pitched brother against brother and father against son. Be that as it may, Venezis had a serious obligation to honor: the archbishop had taken a prominent part in the successful campaign to save the author from execution by the Nazis when they kept him in Block C of Averoff Prison.

The most ambitious of Venezis' journalistic works, *Chronicle of the Bank of Greece* (1955), was written to commemorate the first quarter century of the institution, 1928 to 1952.[3] As a history it represents a more creative labor than does *Archbishop Damaskinos*. The documents are more thoroughly digested, and much more of the text is in the author's own words. Venezis has to summarize and evaluate because twenty-five years in the life of a busy bank can produce an enormous number of primary sources. He has tried to satisfy several major purposes in the book: first, to record the growth of the Bank of Greece in terms of assets and influence; second, to relate the state-owned institution to the historic events which convulsed the nation and the world; third, to examine the bank's continuous effect upon Greece's economy; fourth, to explore the bank's role in the country's external affairs; and fifth, to honor its leading personnel by a series of portraits of directors and lesser executives. Despite the labor expended upon it, *The Chronicle* never rises above the level of journalism.

The relative failure of *The Ocean* (1956) may partly explain why for over a decade Venezis has not published a new novel. What happens in this narrative may be stated simply: not enough. The story line is so thin and its description of places visited by the characters, the crew of the *Manto*, are so elaborate that one can define it as a travelogue disguised as a novel. More action should befall a stronger and more definite protagonist in a book whose laudable purpose is to honor those Greeks who go down to the sea in ships. The dedication reads: "In repayment to Dimitri, 'Captain Papazoglou,' with whom we crossed the Atlantic. To the seamen of the Greek merchant marine who travel the oceans. To the mothers and wives who wait for them." [4] The author takes the *Manto* from Livorno, Italy, to Algeria in North Africa, thence across the Atlantic to Baltimore, Maryland. To honor Greeks as men of the sea, which Venezis does, pays homage to their maritime tradition that goes back to ancient history and merges, through Homer, with heroic myth. As a young boy in Aivali, Venezis acquired a feeling for the sea which has never left him. *The Ocean* is the dramatized log of a tourist who is also a creative artist. The persons, places, and incidents he experiences are recorded as a tribute to his compatriots who leave home and family to sail the seven seas.

II   Archbishop Damaskinos

The book begins with these sad words: "The days of great bitterness for Greece have begun. April of 1940. The Germans have reached Athens, their flag flies on the Acropolis. Greece has fallen, Greece lies in mourning, in blood and in tears." [5] In this hour of defeat, when both the king and the government have gone into exile, only the church remains to protect the nation. The refusal of the previous Archbishop of Athens, Chrysanthos, to serve the collaborationist government of General Tsolakoglou brings Damaskinos to the ecclesiastical throne on July 6, 1941. As bishop and ruler of the church, Damaskinos believes not in the example of the Byzantines but in that of the prelates who fought with the people during the Greek Revolution of 1821–1829. His dilemma is great: to do as his predecessor has done and resign, or to exercise his office as well as possible under the Germans and their Greek puppets. He decides to stay.

Venezis characterizes the archbishop very positively in terms most appealing to the Greek mind. "He comes from the mountains, from the simple, the almost patriarchal life of the shepherds and the woodsmen of mountainous Greece. He comes from the foundations of our people, from the Greek period when belief was not taught but practiced: belief in God, in good deeds, in one's obligation to country and to Greek survival" (p. 13). In his father's modest house Damaskinos gained the pure faith that he kept as theologian and archbishop. From the same strong roots derived the simplicity, the courage, and the dignity that he exhibited to both friend and foe during the difficult days. About him there was nothing false; he was a naturally good man. He had the stature and the mien of a Biblical figure capable of extracting respect even from the German overlords.

With document after document, usually quoted in full, Venezis covers the somewhat more than three years in the life and work of Damaskinos while Archbishop of Athens. He provides enough historical background to make the document, very often a letter written by the archbishop, meaningful to the reader. The first of seven parts is entitled "The Bulgarians in Greece." In the north, in

Eastern Macedonia and Western Thrace, Hitler's Bulgarian allies
sought to eliminate every trace of Hellenism and assure for themselves their long-desired outlet to the Aegean. They persecuted
the clergy of the Greek Orthodox Church; they closed the schools
and forbade the inhabitants to speak Greek; they arrested all
Greek notables and sent them to concentration camps or into
exile; they seized Greek land and brought in thousands of Bulgarian families to occupy the confiscated properties; finally, in October, 1941, they instituted a mass slaughter. It was against these
genocidal atrocities that Archbishop Damaskinos protested in letters to the German ambassador in Athens, Gunther Altenburg.

In the second part, "Famine in Greece," Venezis records what
Archbishop Damaskinos did to discharge the great duty of saving
the people from starvation, caused by the systematic robbery of
their produce by the Germans and Italians. The archbishop asked
the first collaborationist regime of Premier Tsolakoglou that the
church be vested with the task of distributing the available food,
and of acting as intermediary with Turkey and other outside
sources for the purchase of more.

A typical move by the church was an appeal to the Vatican for
help in procuring foodstuffs and the consequent meeting with a
papal representative to discuss the problem. Another was the attempt to send Greek delegates outside the country, to Ankara in
Turkey, for the purpose of arranging for Australian wheat. The
Germans refused permission. Nor was any help forthcoming from
the Vatican as indicated in a letter from Cardinal Maglione to
Premier Themistocles Sophoulis dated October 29, 1941. The terrible winter of 1941–1942 brought severe hunger and tragedy to
Greece. In London the Greek government-in-exile sought aid
from both Churchill and Roosevelt. The suffering intensified.

What may be deemed the heart of the book, "Greek Tragedy,"
is divided into two parts respectively entitled "The First Years"
and "Blood and Tears." After the first difficult year of famine had
passed, a new and even more frightful ordeal descended upon
Greece: the savage retaliation of the German and Italian fascists
against the Resistance which had emerged throughout the nation.
These reprisals seldom affected those who were actually "guilty"
of acts of resistance or sabotage against the Axis forces. "They
[the Occupation forces] blocked entire neighborhoods, they took
hostages and executed them, they burned villages, they killed

whatever crossed their path, they left behind them terror" (p. 179). The fascists punished the nation mercilessly with prison, torture, and killing. After being dragged to the dreaded Gestapo headquarters on Merlin Street, the victims were either shot by firing squads or hanged from trees along the boulevards of Athens. Each morning crowds of frantic suppliants gathered at the archdiocese; they fell to their knees before Archbishop Damaskinos. They begged him to intercede with the enemy, to try to save their doomed loved ones. When he tried and failed, the tragedy of Greece was reflected in his grim face.

To be the spiritual father of the Greek people during the Occupation was, indeed, a most grievous time for Damaskinos of Athens. Under difficult circumstances he used every power of his office to help ease the mass suffering. At the funeral of the great poet Kostis Palamas, who died on February 28, 1942, he gave a memorial to a throng so huge that it was in effect a demonstration of national protest. Venezis in these chapters chronicles many encounters and much correspondence between the archbishop and the hangmen who ruled the country. Especially tragic was the German practice of taking and killing innocent hostages. Archbishop Damaskinos officiated at many sad occasions; for example, the Germans on January 7, 1943, executed fourteen prisoners without announcing their names. The archbishop not only read the names; he also obtained permission to exhume each body for identification and, in the freezing rain, gave each corpse a Christian burial in the presence of the dead man's relatives.

The second part of the section, "Blood and Tears," continues to record the response of Archbishop Damaskinos to the terror of the Occupation. Venezis cites his numerous protests to the Germans and Italians. At one point the Germans asked Damaskinos to condemn the Resistance, but he refused. With every means possible, the church under his aegis helped the families of the executed. Also in this section Venezis devotes a chapter to the fate of the Greek Jews. During the first two years of the Occupation, 1941 and 1942, they were not touched; but from the beginning of 1943 their tragedy started, as it had already begun throughout Europe.

The next section, "Cairo and the Archbishop," examines important aspects of the relationship between Damaskinos in Athens and the Greek Government-in-Exile, brought to Egypt and sustained there by the British. In the first episode an agent from

Cairo, Major John Tsigante, met secretly with Damaskinos in mid-1942 and got his consent to lead a National Resistance Council. It was hoped that the EAM, the National Liberation Front, would agree to come under the archbishop's leadership. The meeting of various Council members was held some months later, on January 7, 1943, a very bad day for Archbishop Damaskinos. He had on that day to read off the names of the fourteen hostages executed by the Germans. On the following day, the Italians killed the agent Tsigante in his hiding place. Thus the Cairo-inspired plan for a National Resistance Council fell through.

Another plan involving the archbishop was the idea, first proposed by the British on October 28, 1943, to have him head a regency committee in the absence of King George, who was living out the war in London. Damaskinos would in effect act as Regent upon liberation and help prepare the way for the return of the king to his throne. King George rejected the plan and agreed only to have a committee act as a trustee of his royal interests in Greece.

Venezis relates how a Colonel Fradellos mistakenly parachuted into EAM-ELAS (Resistance) territory to bring from Cairo the reply regarding the regency plan. After many perils Fradellos reached the archbishop in Athens. More important, perhaps, were the deliberations between the Cairo government of Premier Emanuel Tsouderos and the new popular leaders, some of whom were Communists, brought forth by the people's struggle. In these talks Damaskinos had the vital role of intermediary. It may well be said that the Cold War began in Greece as a result of Winston Churchill's alarm that the EAM-ELAS coalition would establish a socialist system in postwar Greece. It took a bitter civil war, British military intervention, and the Truman Doctrine before the royalist-rightist Establishment could safely be restored.

During the summer of 1944, the terror of the Germans reached its peak as the Resistance, led by EAM-ELAS, spread everywhere and became formidable in the cities as well as the mountains. By this time Archbishop Damaskinos had grown dangerous in the eyes of the enemy. "Days of 1944," the last section in the book, relates his troubles with the Gestapo which began in May and included surveillance, interrogation, and house arrest. While in isolation he received a message from Cairo to the effect that he should escape to the Middle East, but he declined with thanks.

"Should I get up and leave?" he asked. "I who all these years have been urging the Greek people to remain unmoved?" (p. 321). Both Radio Cairo and Radio London protested his detention, yet all summer he remained in virtual custody. Then in September, when it was evident the Germans were preparing to abandon Greece, the guards left his residence. Not long after, on October 12, 1944, the Greek people celebrated their liberation. On that day the sun beat down on the ancient marbles of the Acropolis. Archbishop Damaskinos blessed the gathered multitudes. The book ends with these words: "Thus spoke the archbishop. And the throng, weeping, gave thanks to God" (p. 329).

III   *The Bank of Greece*

In his second historical work, *Chronicle of the Bank of Greece* (1955), Venezis composed a memorial celebrating the first quarter century (1928–1952) of the institution for which he had worked almost since its founding. He retired from his position as Assistant Director in 1957, two years after the *Chronicle* appeared. The book was partly an obligation, partly a means of receiving a well-deserved bonus upon retirement. Greece has other banks, of course, that go back to the early days of the kingdom. This one, the latest, developed during the crisis forced upon the nation by the influx of 1,500,000 refugees from Asia Minor and Eastern Thrace; such was the number of Greeks displaced from their homes after the Catastrophe of 1922. A Financial Committee from the League of Nations visited Greece in 1927 to survey her economic needs created by the massive influx of population. Venezis devotes the first three chapters to the preliminary discussions, correspondence, and agreements leading to the bank's organization in 1928. Briefly noted are the outside financial interests that figured in the founding; also mentioned as having acted in various capacities are names famous in modern Greek history, such as Emanuel Tsouderos, a premier of the Government-in-Exile during the war. The first director of the Bank of Greece was Alexander Diomedes.

In general the book is what it claims to be: a chronicle of the highlights in the first twenty-five years of the bank's existence. One's search for literary quality ends in failure, but for both the economist and the historian the compilation has value. In the bank's life is mirrored, to a considerable extent, the life of the nation itself and, to a lesser degree, of the world. Venezis has to be strictly the journalist here, not the artist, since he does not have the chance even for vivid descriptions. That to the non-economist he seems to be capable of manipulating figures and digesting statistics proves again the wide range of his interests. Nowhere is he a critic of the institution, nor does he attempt any deep objective analysis of the overall impact of the bank upon the economic direction of Greece. To what extent he succeeds or fails in this crucial aspect of the *Chronicle* must be left for the social scientists to determine.

Venezis lists the bank's initial assets, its top managerial personnel, and its immediate problems on the day, May 14, 1928, when it opened its doors for business. A few months later, on December 8th, the Bank of Greece was the principal agent for the arrangement on behalf of the Greek Government of a loan of four million British pounds from Hambros Bank Limited and Erlangers Limited "for public works in Greece and productive purposes." [6]

The bank had hardly begun its operations when the entire world slipped into crisis induced by the financial panic in the United States—the stock market crash of late 1929.

From its beginning, then, the Bank of Greece made vital contributions to the nation's economy. The nature of these contributions changed according to the country's needs, its shifts in domestic and foreign policy, its being at peace or at war. The part called "The Pre-war Years" begins with the abandonment of the gold standard by the United States in 1933 and ends with Hitler's conquest of Czechoslovakia in 1938. This period saw the end of democracy in Greece and the establishment on August 4, 1936, of the fascist regime of General John Metaxas. The period of dictatorship with its economic policies affecting the Bank of Greece merged with the period of the Second World War and, for the nation, its occupation by Germany and Italy.

The next section in the *Chronicle*, "During the War," sums up the history of the bank from 1939 until the end of 1944. Italy invaded Greece in the fall of 1940. At the end of January, 1941, Dictator Metaxas died. That spring a powerful German army invaded and quickly conquered the nation which had successfully resisted the Italian attack. Lest the gold reserves of Greece fall into German hands, they were moved temporarily from Athens to

Crete. Venezis quotes from a director of the bank, George Matzavinos, who wrote years after liberation about the gold movement as well as the exodus from Athens of the royal court of King George, the government of Emanuel Tsouderos, and the bank's top personnel. This flight of Greek officialdom occurred on April 22, 1941, with the aid of two destroyers, the *King George* and the *Queen Olga*. From Crete the Greek leaders went to Egypt. For the duration of the war the gold reserves were kept in the South African Reserve Bank, in Pretoria. To move, store, and insure its gold bullion cost the Bank of Greece the sum of 500,000 pounds.

Within the country the Bank of Greece, suffering under the Occupation, fell within the jurisdiction of the Finance Ministry of the quisling government. The tone of the writing now recalls that of *Archbishop Damaskinos,* in which Venezis talks about tyranny and sorrow. He lists the four collaborationist directors of the bank and their individual tenure. "The occupiers of Greece," he writes, "wanted the Bank of Greece as a basis of attack for the robbery and economic stripping of the nation." [7] To assure this function, the Occupation authorities appointed German and Italian trustees or overseers whose wish was law. They dictated every important policy. The famine which Venezis describes in his other writings affected the employees of the bank as well as everyone else. Their anguish was not lessened, to say the least, because they were working for the enemy.

The economic condition of Greece grew worse as time passed. Venezis recalls that dramatic day, October 28, 1943, when he and others at the bank were arrested by the Gestapo. From this traumatic experience came the play *Block C*. A committee of employees had received permission for a memorial meeting to honor the heroes of the Albanian campaign from the bank's director, Theodore Turkovasili, who was nominally a collaborator. The events that followed—the firing on the assembly by the SS, and the subsequent arrests—have already been described in connection with *Block C*. Venezis writes that the public protest in behalf of the prisoners, including himself, constituted the first resistance action of the Greeks against the Germans.

The last section of the *Chronicle*, "The Postwar Years," brings to a conclusion the author's resumé of the bank's first quarter century. At the end of this period, 1952, the bank had long been established as one of the country's major organizations. After liberation in 1944, the truly national administration of the bank, led by its authentic director, Kyriakos Barbaresos, returned from exile to resume old duties and to rebuild, on new fiscal foundations, what the war had shattered. Venezis catalogues the growing role of the bank in the era of the Marshall Plan and postwar reconstruction. The year 1950 saw the last great world event in this period, the outbreak of the Korean War, which impinged significantly upon the Greek economy. It did so due to decreased American aid and the resulting cutback on programs predicated on such aid.

The *Chronicle* in its entirety is a testimony to the sensitive responses of a great national bank to the domestic and foreign crises that befell the country. This correlation comes through even for the reader who is not thoroughly versed in the complicated languages of economics and finance. For such a reader the *Chronicle of the Bank of Greece* has limited appeal; but for the scholar and historian Venezis has done some of the preliminary work of sifting sources, highlighting relevant events, and establishing their impact upon the institution to which he gave so much of his life.

IV A Novel about the Sea

Elias Venezis learned to love the sea while a youth in Aivali, Turkey. There, as is the wont of boys, he watched the ships come and go at the harbor. *The Ocean* begins at the end of the war with the liberty ship, the *Manto,* having just brought a load of coal from Norfolk, Virginia, to Livorno, Italy. Conversing with other shipmates in the ship's mess, Captain Joachim recalls the year 1940 and his last trip to Japan on another ship with a load of scrap iron from Mexico. While en route west of Honolulu they heard that Greece had been invaded by Italy. They had put in at Manila until assured that their ship would not be impounded. Returning from Japan, they had gotten oil in Borneo and coal in Calcutta for the Greek Government. The Greeks of Calcutta gave them many gifts: ambulances, bandages, boot leather, wool. The ship reached the port of Piraeus and unloaded just after an aerial bombardment; several days later the ship was sunk. Listening to the captain's tale is an apprentice mechanic of nineteen on his first voyage The older secretary asks, "Are you sure you want to live on the sea? Why did you choose the sea?" The answer from the youth is that in Greece life on the land is hard. He will try the sea.[8]

The aged steward Nicholas, while gazing off at the harbor of Livorno, notices below him on the wharf two youths of about fourteen, a boy and a girl. Both, as it turns out, were orphaned by the wartime bombardment of Livorno. The boy's name is Elias; he is a Jew, born in Smyrna, who speaks a little Greek. The girl is Italian. She carries a cage with a bird inside trained to pick up fortune cards with its beak; no doubt it is the same girl as in *Autumn in Italy*. Nicholas invites them aboard where he feeds them and learns something of their past. To the girl he gives a packet of sugar cubes. On the card which the bird picks for Nicholas is a girl with her eyes blindfolded. She stands for luck. The children admonish the steward always to carry the card with him, and all will be well.

When Nicholas asks them to guide him about Livorno, Elias takes him to his hovel in the ruins and offers him the young girl for sex. "You gave her sugar. She wants to repay you. You do not want?" (p. 27). Nicholas is overwhelmed with sadness for the orphans in their desperate need. And he weeps at the memory of his own child, a girl, killed in the bombardment of Piraeus in the early days of the war.

The second lieutenant of the *Manto*, Vasilis, is a strong young man of twenty-eight who speaks with the apprentice mechanic about his island, Andros. He has not seen the island for four years. They look off at a little island which Vasilis claims is named "The Gorgon" after the ancient myth about Alexander the Great. The gorgon brings good luck to sailors. Vasilis listens eagerly to the apprentice telling of a recent stopover at Andros when the women were allowed to join their menfolk aboard the ship. Vasilis differs from the rest of the crew in that he never carouses ashore, never gets drunk or rolled. He has the dream of returning to Andros. He gets the apprentice to accompany him to Montenero, a mountain near Livorno with a church at its summit reached by a funicular. They visit the beautiful place as tourists. The account at this point reads like a travelogue; Venezis devotes about three pages of description to the scene. The Greek seamen cross themselves in the church. Vasilis tells the apprentice to imagine they are on Andros.

On board the *Manto* the boy Elias helps the cook, who is from

Samos, and gets the leftovers in return. Elias begs his friend Nicholas to help him stow away as far as North Africa. At first Nicholas refuses, but finally consents and hides Elias in his own cabin.
On the following day the empty *Manto* leaves the port of Livorno
bound for Bone in Algeria to receive cargo for America. Venezis
describes the ship's departure and mentions in the crew's dialogue
the various places they pass: Gorgon, Elba, Corsica, Cape Corso.
It is impossible, of course, for him to particularize more than a
very few characters. Not one character, in fact, is adequately developed, not even the stowaway Elias, mainly because the plot is
determined by theme and not by one sustained action. Too much
of the dialogue, for example, stems from the external geography
of the passage instead of the inner necessities of the crew; and too
many characters are introduced, not in order to further a systematic plot, but to round out a gallery of seafaring types. Either that,
or to express segments of ideology such as the statement upon
departure, "All is real, simple and strong. The sea. God. Greece"
(p. 53). Also brought out is the aim of many to ship out and save
enough money to settle down somewhere on land, back home or
else in some other highly romanticized place. More often than not,
the hope is vain.

A major reason for the vanity of this pervasive wish is illustrated when the *Manto* docks in Algeria. Here again Venezis gives
much travelogue-type description, as if to answer the question,
"What's it like in Africa, among the Arabs?" He shows the crew
wasting their money in dives, getting drunk, arrested, and rolled
by whores. Between themselves and their dream for a landed
haven comes their hunger for excitement, for love. Venezis, again
a tourist, pauses at sights of interest: an Arab funeral, the streets
named after famous Frenchmen, Ramadan. The strongest thread
of story deals with Elias; he leaves the *Manto* with his benefactor
Nicholas who has many regrets for having brought him along.
They see blind beggars and drunks. They pass through narrow
dark alleys, and enter a dive. The poverty and despair remind
Elias of Livorno. Nicholas promises to feed him until the *Manto*
leaves for America.

Just before the vessel leaves, with Elias stowed away in a life-
boat, Venezis depicts a most dramatic scene: the enticement of
the crew by three whores who appear on the dock. One bares her
bosom to the seamen, the other shows her legs. The frantic men

leap down and take the women behind the piled cargo; in the eyes of the moral Vasili, this is added proof of how the sea turns men into rot. More proof is furnished by a Finnish seaman who begs to be taken aboard, but is refused; he had missed his own ship because of drunkenness. He appears in the story, "A Finn in Algiers."

After the *Manto* passes Gibraltar, Elias is discovered and brought before the first in command, Captain John, who beats him to learn who helped him stow away. The old steward admits that he is to blame. Later, in the chart room, the captain records the incident in the ship's log. Elias becomes the cook's helper. Nicholas ponders his fate; he will return to the mud of Thessaly and will tell of a deed (his aiding Elias) that had neither purpose nor gain.

Three days out in the Atlantic, the crew talk of many things. Their memories become brief flashbacks that fill in the slow time. It rains, there may be a storm, they approach the Gulf Stream. Venezis mentions hardly any political discussion, a fact which seems odd in view of the civil war in Greece and the widespread radicalism of the Greek seamen. He does mythologize at length about the Gulf Stream, this "hot river within the Atlantic." In the eyes of the crew it has a peculiar dynamism; it stands for fate and death. Anything can happen in the Gulf Stream. In its heat men squabble and fight. It is here, on this trip, that Nicholas goes mad, here among the seaweed floating up from the West Indies. Nobody goes to see him; the captain has a superstition about death aboard his ship. Even the boy Elias avoids him. The Gulf Stream also intensifies desire, as illustrated by a Puerto Rican member of the crew who eagerly looks forward to his green-eyed girlfriend in New York. Stripped to the waist, he resembles a demon as he goes about the boat. Soon the *Manto* nears the Bermudas. They see gulls and flying fish.

The dialogue of the novel now deals with the final stages of the voyage; their destination looms and affects the crew in various ways. In fact, the destination constitutes the only unifying theme for the characters who have been singled out for emphasis. The course of the *Manto*, originally set for New York, shifts to Baltimore. "There where Edgar Allen Poe rests" (p. 229). At last Captain John visits the dying Nicholas who fails to respond when spoken to. The stowaway boy Elias worries about his future until a friend of Nicholas, the "Ximantzis," a former dealer in wholesale goods, invites Elias to retire with him to Thessaly. There the "Ximantzis" will drive a steamroller and gaze down all day at the earth; one cannot be lost when he is buried in his own soil. Captain John, in a race with death, is increasingly impatient to reach Baltimore. The crew had been very animated when the *Manto* first entered the Gulf Stream; now, as they leave, they hardly give it a thought. Then, the lighthouse of Chesapeake Bay! Their long and lonely journey is nearly over; it has taken them fourteen days.

"What is the *Manto?*" Venezis asks in the final chapter. The reader has known her as a converted Liberty Ship; she carries 10,000 tons of cargo. Wall Street ordered her course changed to Baltimore. Her captain hails from Andros, but he will never return there. The *Manto*'s second in command, Joachim, has lost his post as captain; he, too, may never return to a landed haven. Vasili, the strong and pure in heart, now dresses neatly for the shore. He has strong roots, he will not rot like the others. He, too, is from Andros; yet he finds Andros everywhere he goes—even in Baltimore. Elias, the orphan of war, will go to Thessaly to begin a new life with his latest benefactor, the "Ximantzis." Also dressed neatly, the Puerto Rican finds his lady waiting for him on the dock—but her eyes are not green. Real women differ from the ocean dreams of sailors. The old steward Nicholas, still breathing, is carried out. "Thank God we brought him alive," Captain John says. "He will not die on the *Manto*. Let him go down the stairs of the *Manto* and die in port" (p. 274). On this somber note, with the boat quietly anchored, the story ends.

In this least effective of his novels, Venezis has a very laudable aim: to honor the sailors of the Greek merchant marine, of whom there are no seadogs more brave, more resourceful, or more Odyssean. *The Ocean* has characters who, if adequately developed in action, could be memorable. It has a setting, broad and suitable for any mood, that would have gained greatly in significance had it served for more than a routine crossing of the Atlantic. Finally, the novel has a theme: how a boat like the *Manto* gathers a variety of fates, of Greek types; yet even a plot of theme must have a compelling and unifying action out of which the theme grows, in the way that effect grows from cause and symbol from object. In short, *The Ocean* lacks plot in the formal sense of the term. The only unifying factors are the sea itself, the *Manto,* the crossing, and the several characters who appear and reappear; yet even these major characters are too thinly presented for the reader really to know them. According to one critic, the sea in *The Ocean* is something more than geography. "The sea here is not simply a physical environment in which is placed the action of the heroes of the work. It determines also the function of the characters, their conscience, their soul." [9] The good ship *Manto* crosses the Atlantic in order to give the author a chance briefly to sketch a gallery of types that generally man the Greek merchant marine. Aside from providing such a gallery, which may be interesting in itself, *The Ocean* as a novel accomplishes very little.

V   *The Journalist*

Prolific in the genres already noted, Venezis has also written extensively for magazines and newspapers. In the years from 1953 to 1965, for example, he had over fifty pieces published in *Nea Estia,* the leading literary journal of Greece. In addition he has written, among other things, a weekly column on "Life and Thought" for the Athens newspaper *Acropolis.* Many of his short stories have enjoyed magazine publication both before and after appearing in book-length collections.

Nea Estia also printed in this period two radio dramas, *The Prisoners of Tripolitsa* and *Above the Flames.*[10] The first goes back to an event in the Greek Revolution and dramatizes the escape of a religious leader, called "Metropolitan Daniel" in the play, from a Turkish prison. The second, *Above the Flames,* exploits the Catastrophe of 1922 and its aftermath. The stage directions mention the exodus of Greeks to the island of Lesbos in 1924. Actually, Venezis dramatizes two short stories that deal with the Turkish character Akif. In the play Akif's son Achmed becomes a Christian at Easter and marries the Greek girl Maria, the daughter of old Uncle Stathis.

The many other articles from *Nea Estia* may best be discussed by grouping them into various categories. The largest single type consists of memorials to dead writers and other intellectuals. These are rather short eulogies that contain much fine praise but no real critical evaluation. Some of the persons memorialized have a worldwide reputation, but most are famous only within Greece. Among the former is the American novelist Ernest Hemingway.[11] Now, Venezis writes, the bells are tolling for Hemingway himself.

The two Greeks of world stature are Anghelos Sikelianos, the poet, and Dmitri Mitropoulos, the conductor. What he declares about Sikelianos, including his visit to Delphi, is reproduced in the travelogue The Argonauts.[12] Mitropoulos, Venezis points out, was the first artist of the postwar period to give Greece an international reputation in music.[13] Even before Pearl Harbor he was the regular conductor for the Minneapolis Symphony.

Another category of journalistic pieces deals with books, authors, and other aesthetic subjects. In one Venezis speaks of the fame of Hans Christian Andersen in Greece; he does so while also writing about his friend Carsten Höeg, the Danish Philhellene. In a travel article Venezis describes his visit to the house of Dostoyevsky, just outside of Moscow. There he examines the manuscript of The Brothers Karamazov.[14] In another he journeys to the island of Rhodes where he reports upon the performance of a play. When the editor of Nea Estia goes on a European tour, Venezis edits three issues of the magazine. As a result he comments on his difficulties, on the "nightmare duties" of an editor.[15]

Speaking about one of his own ancestors in "A Case of Piracy in the Aegean," Venezis writes most interestingly about a George Mellos, a trader of the late 17th century, whose ship the Saint George was captured by two Venetian pirate vessels on May 6, 1678. Mellos went to the Duchess of Savoy to demand justice, but was denied. Thereafter he went to Madrid where he gained great wealth in trade, thence to Venice where he died very wealthy at the age of 85. Venezis shows how the forbears of the Aegean archipelago had been dominated by so many—Turks, Algerians, Maltese, Franks, the dukes of Savoy, pirates and nobles—"monsters all." [16]

A final important category (not to mention more isolated topics) concerns national and patriotic issues. At this level Venezis speaks more directly to the people as a member of the Academy. For example, he introduces a special issue of Nea Estia to "OXI," the classic "NO" of defiance which Greece issued to Italy before war broke out in 1940.[17] At least four of his patriotic articles deal with the more immediate question of Cyprus. One sadly reports, in 1955, that the first martyr of Cyprus, a youth, has just been killed on the island.[18] A second is a letter signed by Venezis and sent to three English writers on the problem of ENOSIS, the union of Cyprus with Greece.[19] In a third, "The Annunciation of

1956," on the occasion of March 25th (Greek Independence Day), Venezis stresses the patriotic note by declaring: "Acropolis, our hope, spirit of Hellenism, spirit of our passion for Freedom and Beauty and Man, now in these days of 1956, one hundred and thirty-five years after the days of '21, now that again we suffer as a nation, we wish to appeal to you." [20] The fourth Cyprus article bitterly assails the Turkish atrocities against Greeks and the Orthodox churches in Istanbul and elsewhere; to Venezis these are the days of 1922 all over again.[21]

The author's one persistent national concern has been to establish in Greece a system of conservation similar to the National Parks in the United States. Some progress has indeed been made in that direction. Venezis has also led in the movement to protect monuments of the past. On both these related issues he has spoken and written at some length; to him the Greek landscape has almost a sacred meaning.[22] In the article "The Uprooted Greeks" Venezis reports on a symposium held on this historic subject; he himself, one may recall, falls within this class due to the expulsion of his family from Asia Minor.[23] In "The Foreign Thinkers," he stresses the peculiar advantage of Greece concerning her image, brought about by the fact that many intellectuals abroad think very highly of her traditions.[24] Greece has a great reserve of good will on which she can depend in future years.

Venezis recalls elsewhere, in "The Old Man of Macedonia," an article about a teacher, that the last act of the Athens Academy in 1954 was to grant him an award. Finally, in "The Premier Speaks," Venezis prints an interview with George Papandreou held in 1960 during which the grand old man of Greek liberal politics, out of office then and dispirited, wished to discuss Art, the Theater, and Thought.[25] In the interesting dialogue Venezis quotes from the political leader a statement with which he can readily agree: "The Greek laurel is bitter." Underlying the most valuable writings of Venezis is the related thought: life in Greece is tragic.

This brief discussion of his typical journalistic endeavors rounds out and completes the career of Venezis as an outstanding man of letters. He has not published any poetry or satire or humor; but he has produced in so many literary genres, and has excelled in so many individual works, that he may be placed among such contemporary masters of prose as Stratis Myrivilis, Anghelos Terzakis, and perhaps even with the greatest master of all, Nikos Kazantzakis. In our view the lasting fame of Venezis will rest not on his dramas or histories or travelogues but on a select group of his short stories and on three of his novels, *Number 31328*, *Serenity*, and *Beyond the Aegean*. Any one of these works would be sufficient to warrant him significant mention in the history of Greek literature. That he has reached so many peaks as well as plateaus of excellence makes him worthy of the title he proudly bears, "Elias Venezis, member of the Athens Academy."

Notes and References

Chapter One

1. G. Valetas, *Anthology of Demotic Prose Writers,* III, 1888–1922 (Athens, 1949), pp. 577–664.

2. An entire volume devoted to the group is Andreas Karandonis, *Prose Writers and Prose Works of the Generation of 1930* (Athens, 1962).

3. A reference in English to the "generation of 1930" may be found in George G. Arnakis, "The Tragedy of Man in the Poetry of George Seferis," *Texas Quarterly,* VII (Spring, 1964), pp. 55–67.

4. The review explaining the play's failure was written by Drassos Kastanakis in *Free Letters* (December 21, 1945), p. 13.

5. Nikos Kazantzakis, *Japan: China* (New York, 1963).

6. Other honors bestowed upon Venezis include the National Literary Award, 1939; Athenian Academy Award, 1939; and a travel grant to the United States under provisions of the Smith-Mundt Act, 1949.

7. In letter from Venezis dated June 21, 1966.

8. A. W. Gomme, *Greece* (London, New York, Toronto, 1945).

9. *Ibid.,* p. 62.

10. *Ibid.,* pp. 62–63.

11. The version of "Manolis Lekas" used is from *Winds* (Athens, 1944), pp. 127–57. The following page numbers refer to the same source.

12. Venezis usually revised succeeding editions of his works. The following resumé of *Number 31328* is from the fourth edition (Athens, 1959). The first edition appeared in 1931.

13. *Ibid.,* p. 23. The following page numbers refer to the same source.

14. Andreas Karandonis, *Prose Writers and Prose Works of the Generation of 1930,* pp. 129–30.

15. Stratis Loukas, *Story of a Captive* (Athens, 1929).

16. From excerpt inside front cover, fourth edition, *Number 31328,* 1959.

17. Henri Liebrecht, "Number 31328 of Elias Venezis," *ibid.,* p. 11.

18. From excerpt on back cover, *ibid.*

19. *Ibid.*

20. From excerpt inside front cover, *ibid.*

21. From excerpt inside back cover, *ibid.*

22. Georges Lecompte, in letter praising the French translation of *Number 31328, ibid.,* p. 9.

23. Liebrecht, *op. cit.,* p. 11.

24. From excerpt inside back cover, *ibid.*

25. Venezis, "Author's Prologue to the Second Edition," *ibid.,* p. 12.

26. Apostolos Sahinis, "The Fiction of Elias Venezis," *The Charioteer,* I (Autumn, 1960), p. 86.

Chapter Two

1. Venezis, *Serenity,* 9th ed. (Athens, 1956). The first edition of *Serenity* appeared in 1939. In the 1956 edition Venezis made "substantial changes" in diction and rhythm.

2. Venezis, *Beyond the Aegean.* Tr. from the Greek by E. D. Scott-Kilvert (New York, 1957).

3. Venezis, *Serenity,* p. 12. The following page numbers refer to the same source.

4. John Hatzinis, "The Characters of Elias Venezis," *Greek Works* (Athens, n.d.), p. 125.

5. Nikos Kazantzakis, *The Greek Passion* (New York, 1954).

6. Venezis, *Exodus* (Athens, 1950).

7. Lawrence Durrell, "Preface," *Beyond the Aegean,* vi.

8. Venezis, *Beyond the Aegean,* 1. The following page numbers refer to the same source.

9. Anghelos Sikelianos, "Prologue of Anghelos Sikelianos for the Second Edition of *Beyond the Aegean," Beyond the Aegean,* 6th ed. (Athens, 1965), p. 13.

10. Durrell, *op. cit.,* p. v. The following page numbers refer to the same source.

11. Pierre Amandry, "Prologue of Pierre Amandry for the French Edition," *Beyond the Aegean,* 6th ed. (Athens, 1965), p. 20.

12. Hatzinis, *Greek Works,* p. 128.

13. From excerpt inside front cover, *Beyond the Aegean,* 6th ed. (Athens, 1965).

14. *Ibid.*

15. From excerpt inside back cover, *ibid.*

16. *Ibid.*

Chapter Three

1. Venezis, *The Aegean,* 2nd ed. (Athens, 1948). All stories summarized here are from this edition.

2. Karandonis, *Prose Writers and Prose Works of the Generation of 1930,* p. 136.

3. "Lios" first appeared in *Manolis Lekas* (Athens, 1928). *Nea Estia* reprinted "Lios" as Venezis' favorite story, 70 (September 1, 1961), pp. 1149–59.

4. "Lios," *The Aegean*, p. 19.

5. See Chapter One for more on the population exchange.

6. "Akif," *The Aegean*, p. 79. The following page numbers refer to the same source.

7. *Above the Flames*, a radio play written by Venezis at Easter, 1962, for the fortieth anniversary of the Asia Minor catastrophe. It concern the marriage of Akif's son to the Christian girl Maria. Its final scene symbolizes peaceful reconciliation of Greek and Turk. *Nea Estia*, 71 (May 1, 1962), pp. 564–69.

8. "The Seagulls," *The Aegean*, p. 54. This story, translated by Robert Liddell and Constantine Trypanis, appeared in *The Atlantic Monthly*, 195 (June, 1955), pp. 117–119.

9. "The Roar," *The Aegean*, p. 88.

10. I. M. Panayotopoulos, *Writers and Their Works*, II, "The Restless Years" (Athens, 1943), p. 70.

11. "The Bird," *The Aegean*, p. 102.

12. "Tale of the Aegean," *The Aegean*, p. 178.

13. Karandonis, *Prose Writers and Prose Works of the Generation of 1930*, p. 134.

14. "The Roar," *The Aegean*, p. 83.

15. Karandonis, *Prose Writers and Prose Works of the Generation of 1930*, p. 136.

16. Venezis, *Winds*, 1st ed. (Athens, 1944).

17. Karandonis, *Prose Writers and Prose Works of the Generation of 1930*, p. 130.

18. *Theonichos U. Mnesarete* (Stuttgart, 1948).

19. See Chapter Seven for reference to *Above the Flames*.

20. "In the Kimindenia," *Winds*, p. 121. The following page numbers refer to the same source.

21. "The Final Hour," *Winds*, p. 17. The following page numbers refer to the same source.

22. "Byzantium, Tokyo, and Andros," *Winds*, 3rd ed. (Athens, no date), p. 144.

23. "Death," *Winds*, p. 106. This and the following references to *Winds* are from the 1st edition.

24. "Theonichos and Mnisarete," *Winds*, p. 24. The following page number refers to the same source.

25. Panayotopoulos, *Writers and Their Works*, p. 65.

26. "Mycenae," *Winds*, p. 51. The following page numbers refer to the same source.

27. "Mount of Olives," *Winds*, p. 94. The following page numbers refer to the same source.

28. See Chapter One for more on the Turkish labor batallions.

29. "Moment on the Saroniko," *Winds*, p. 67. The following page number refers to the same source.

30. Karandonis, *Prose Writers and Prose Works of the Generation of 1930*, p. 137.

Chapter Four

1. Venezis, *Block C* (Athens, 1946). The edition used here bears the copyright date of 1963.

2. In a letter from Venezis dated June 21, 1966.

3. Venezis and L. Koukoulas, "Greek Intellectuals and the Drama of the Occupation," *Free Press*, 4 (June 2, 1945), pp. 3, 15.

4. See Chapter Seven.

5. Venezis and L. Koukoulas, *op. cit.*, p. 3.

6. *Ibid.*

7. Venezis, *Block C*. The following page numbers refer to the same source.

8. For a fuller account of the changing politics of the period see L. S. Stavrianos, *Greece: American Dilemma and Opportunity* (Chicago, 1952).

9. Drassos Kastanakis, "E. Venezis: Block C, National Theater," *Free Letters* (December 21, 1945), p. 13.

10. *Ibid.*, p. 14.

11. *Ibid.*

12. Pellos Katsellis, "Director's Note," *Block C*, p. 15.

13. *Ibid.*, pp. 17–18.

14. *Ibid.*, p. 18.

15. *Ibid.*, *passim.*, pp. 20–25.

16. Venezis, "Note," *Block C*, p. 11. The following page numbers refer to the same source.

17. Venezis, *Exodus* (Athens, 1950), p. 17. The edition used here is the 2nd and bears the copyright date of 1964. The following page numbers refer to the same source.

18. Stavrianos, *Greece*, p. 65.

19. *Ibid.*

Chapter Five

1. Venezis, *Wartime* (Athens, 1946).

2. "People of the Saroniko," *Wartime*, p. 31. The following page numbers refer to the same source.

3. "Tourkolimano," *Wartime*, p. 86. The following page numbers refer to the same source.

4. Venezis, *The Defeated* (Athens, 1954).

5. "The Two Women and the Tower," *The Defeated*, p. 25.

6. "The Shadows of Phaistos" appeared in *Nea Estia*, 75 (January 1, 1964), pp. 8–12.

7. "The Old Man of the Seine and the Three," *The Defeated*, p. 117.

8. "The Broken Branch," *The Defeated*, pp. 45–46. The following page number refers to the same source.

9. "The Knife of Bataan and the Verses," *The Defeated*, p. 63. The following page numbers refer to the same source.

10. "The Bandit Pancho Villa," *The Defeated*, p. 136. The following page numbers refer to the same source.

11. "The Immigrant of Grand Canyon," *The Defeated*, p. 131. The following page numbers refer to the same source.

12. "A Finn in Algiers," *The Defeated*, p. 124.

13. "The State of Virginia," *The Defeated*, p. 20.

14. "The Home of the Lost Angels," *The Defeated*, pp. 111–112.

15. "The Defeated Man and the Raven," *The Defeated*, p. 169.

16. Hatzinis, *Greek Works*, p. 138.

17. "Days of Crete," *The Defeated*, p. 38.

Chapter Six

1. Venezis, *Autumn in Italy* (Athens, 1950).

2. *Ibid.*, p. 10.

3. *Time*, 21 (October 24, 1949), p. 636.

4. Excerpt from inside front cover, *America* (Athens, 1955).

5. Venezis, *The Argonauts* (Athens, 1962).

6. Venezis, *Autumn in Italy*, p. 27. The following page numbers refer to the same source.

7. Venezis, *America*, p. 18. The following page numbers refer to the same source.

8. Venezis, *The Argonauts*, p. 12. The following page numbers refer to the same source.

Chapter Seven

1. Venezis, "The Old Man of Macedonia," *Nea Estia*, 63 (January 1, 1958), p. 411.

2. Venezis, *Archbishop Damaskinos* (Athens, 1952).

3. Venezis, *Chronicle of the Bank of Greece* (Athens, 1955).

4. Venezis, *The Ocean* (Athens, 1956), no page.

5. Venezis, *Archbishop Damaskinos*, p. 2. The following page numbers refer to the same source.

6. Venezis, *Chronicle of the Bank of Greece*, p. 72.

7. *Ibid.*, p. 280.

8. Venezis, *The Ocean*, p. 17. The following page numbers refer to the same source.

9. Editorial Note, *Nea Estia*, 59 (May 1, 1956), p. 601.

10. Venezis, *The Prisoners of Tripolitsa*, *Nea Estia*, 69 (March 15, 1961), pp. 359–64; and *Above the Flames, ibid.*, 71 (May 1, 1962), pp. 564–69. Footnotes 10 to 25 all refer to articles written by Venezis and published in *Nea Estia*. Only the titles, volume number, date, and page will be given.

11. "For Whom the Bell Tolls," 70 (July 15, 1961), pp. 915–17.

12. "In Memory of Anghelos Sikelianos," 56 (July 1, 1954), pp. 978–84.

13. "Memorial for Mitropoulos," 69 (January 1, 1961), pp. 36–37.

14. "In the House of Dostoyevsky," 74 (October 15, 1963), pp. 1346–48.

15. "The Fate of 'Nea Estia,'" 60 (September 15, 1956), pp. 1240–41.

16. "A Case of Piracy in the Aegean," 78 (November 1, 1965), p. 1433.

17. "The Days of 1940," 56 (November 1, 1954), p. 1537.

18. "The Youth of Cyprus," 58 (November 1, 1955), p.1394.

19. [With Petros Haris], "Greek Writers and Cyprus," 56 (August 15, 1954), pp. 1202–04.

20. "The Annunciation of 1956," 59 (April 1, 1956), p. 422.

21. "Tuesday, September 6, 1955," 58 (September 15, 1955), p. 1183.

22. "The Greek Landscape, Its Monuments and Their Protection," 65 (January 1, 1959), pp. 10–11; and "The Pan-Athenian Stadium," 65 (June 1, 1959), p. 751.

23. "The Uprooted Greeks," 61 (May 15, 1957), pp. 691–93.

24. "The Foreign Thinkers," 62 (September 15, 1957), pp. 1344–45.

25. "The Premier Speaks," 77 (January 15, 1965), pp. 103–7.

Selected Bibliography

Books by Elias Venezis

Manolis Lekas. Athens: No publisher given. 1928.
Number 31328. Athens: John D. Kollarou & Company, 1931.
Serenity (Yalini). Athens: John D. Kollarou & Company, 1939.
The Aegean (Aigaio). Athens: Greek Editions, 1941.
Beyond the Aegean (Aioliki Yi). Athens: John D. Kollarou & Company, 1943.
Beyond the Aegean (American edition). Tr. by E. D. Scott-Kilvert. New York: The Vanguard Press, 1957.
Winds (Anemoi). Athens: John D. Kollarou & Company, 1944.
Block C. Athens: John D. Kollarou & Company, 1944.
Wartime (Ora Polemou). Athens: Friends of Books, 1946.
Autumn in Italy. Athens: I. M. Skazikis, 1950.
Exodus. Athens: John D. Kollarou & Company, 1950.
Archbishop Damaskinos. Athens: I. M. Skazikis, 1952.
The Defeated (Oi Nikemenoi). Athens: John D. Kollarou & Company, 1954.
Chronicle of the Bank of Greece. Athens: Bank of Greece, 1955.
America (Amerikaniki Yi). Athens: John D. Kollarou & Company, 1955.
The Ocean (Okeanos). Athens: John D. Kollarou & Company, 1956.
The Argonauts. Athens: John D. Kollarou & Company, 1962.

Other Writings by Venezis

[With L. Koukoulas] "Greek Intellectuals and the Drama of the Occupation," *Free Press (Elefthera Grammata)*, 4 (June 2, 1945), pp. 3, 15.
"The Seagulls." Tr. by Robert Liddell and Constantine Trypanis, *The Atlantic Monthly*, 195 (June, 1955), pp. 117–19.
"Author's Prologue to the Second Edition," *Number 31328.* 4th edition. Athens: John D. Kollarou & Company, 1959.
"Note." *Block C.* Athens: John D. Kollarou & Company, 1946, pp. 11–14.

The following writings by Venezis appeared in *Nea Estia*.

"The True Glory," 55 (May 1, 1954), pp. 588–589.

"In Memory of Anghelos Sikelianos," 56 (July 1, 1954), pp. 978–84.

[With Petros Haris] "Greek Writers and Cyprus," 56 (August 15, 1954), pp. 1202–4.

"The Days of 1940," 56 (November 1, 1954), p. 1537.

"Tuesday, September 6, 1955," 58 (September 15, 1955), p. 1183.

"The Youth of Cyprus," 58 (November 1, 1955), p. 1394.

"The Annunciation of 1956," 59 (April 1, 1956), pp. 421–22.

"An Offering to Santorini," 60 (August 1, 1956), pp. 1031–33.

"The Fate of 'Nea Estia,' " 60 (September 15, 1956), pp. 1240–41.

"The Uprooted Greeks," 61 (May 15, 1957), pp. 691–93.

"The Foreign Thinkers," 62 (September 15, 1957), pp. 1344–45.

"The Old Man of Macedonia," 63 (January 1, 1958), pp. 10–11.

"The Ancestors," 63 (March 15, 1958), pp. 411–12.

"The Greek Landscape, Its Monuments and Their Protection," 65 (January 1, 1959), pp. 10–11.

"The Pan-Athenian Stadium," 65 (June 1, 1959), p. 751.

"The End of a Cephalonian Legend," 67 (April 15, 1960), pp. 505–6.

"Memorial for Mitropoulos," 69 (January 1, 1961), pp. 36–37.

"The Prisoners of Tripolitsa," 69 (March 15, 1961), pp. 359–64.

"For Whom the Bell Tolls," 70 (July 15, 1961), pp. 915–17.

"Lios," 70 (September 1, 1961), pp. 1149–59.

"Above the Flames," 71 (May 1, 1962), pp. 564–69.

"In the House of Dostoyevsky," 74 (October 15, 1963), pp.1346–48.

"The Premier Speaks," 77 (January 15, 1965), pp. 103–7.

"A Case of Piracy in the Aegean," 78 (November 1, 1965), pp. 1430–33.

SECONDARY SOURCES

AMANDRY, PIERRE. "Prologue of Pierre Amandry for the French Edition," *Beyond the Aegean*. 6th edition. Athens: John D. Kollarou & Company, 1965, pp. 17–20. In his prologue the French critic briefly outlines the circumstances which uprooted the Anatolian Greeks both in 1914 and in 1922. He gives a resumé of the contents of the novel. He also states that no book published in modern Greece has enjoyed a comparable popular success.

ARNAKIS, GEORGE G. "The Tragedy of Man in the Poetry of George Seferis." *Texas Quarterly*, VII (Spring, 1954), 55–67. Although of primary interest to students of Seferis, this article helps to establish Venezis as a member of the "Generation of 1930."

DURRELL, LAWRENCE. "Preface." *Beyond the Aegean*. New York: The Vanguard Press, 1957, pp. v–vii. The writer stresses the spirit of the novel more than its content. In doing so, he speaks of the Anatolia as a lost Garden of Eden destroyed forever by persistent war.

GOMME, A. W. *Greece.* London, New York, Toronto: The Oxford University Press, 1945. The book traces the history of modern Greece from the Revolution of 1921 until 1945. It gives a lucid and objective account of the distraught period which one finds reflected in the works of Venezis.

HARIS, PETROS and VENEZIS, ELIAS. "Greek Writers and Cyprus," *Nea Estia,* 56 (August 15, 1954), pp. 1202–1204.

HATZINIS, JOHN. *Greek Works.* Athens: Editions K.M., 1955. In this volume two useful chapters on Greek letters in the first half of the 20th century and symbolism in new Greek prose preface essays on twelve writers. They include Palamas, Cavafy, Kazantzakis, Myrivilis, Venezis, Xenopoulos, and Skipis. In the essay "The Characters of Elias Venezis" (pp. 125–138) the author discusses *Serenity, Beyond the Aegean, Exodus,* and *The Defeated.*

KARANDONIS, ANDREAS. *Prose Writers and Prose Works of the Generation of 1930.* Athens: Y. Fexi, 1962. One of the leading critics of Greece has written in this book a series of essays on thirteen important prose writers who first gained literary prominence in or about the year 1930. Among them are Myrivilis, Terzakis, Theotokas, Kastanakis, and Venezis. The essay on Venezis, dated 1946, is quite short and general.

KASTANAKIS, DRASSOS. "E. Venezis: Block C, National Theater." *Free Letters* (December 21, 1945), p. 13. In this review the critic severely takes the National Theater to task for putting on a poor performance of *Block C.*

KATSELLIS, PELLOS. "Director's Note." *Block C.* Athens: John D. Kollarou & Company, 1946, pp. 15–25. The person who directed *Block C* for the National Theater makes an extended analysis of the special dramaturgical problems encountered in the production of the play.

KAZANTZAKIS, NIKOS. *The Greek Passion.* New York: Simon and Shuster, 1954.

——. *Japan: China.* New York: Simon and Schuster, 1963.

KOUKOULAS, L. and VENEZIS, ELIAS. "Greek Intellectuals and the Drama of the Occupation." *Free Press,* 4 (June 2, 1945), pp. 3, 15. In this interview Venezis is given the chance to discuss not only the drama in general but also his play *Block C.*

LECOMPTE, GEORGES. Letter in Prologue. *Number 31328.* 4th edition. Athens: John D. Kollarou & Company, 1959, pp. 9–10. In his brief letter Lecompte, a member of the French Academy, has great praise for the French translation which appeared under the title, *La Grande Pitié.*

LIEBRECHT, HENRI. "Number 31328 of Elias Venezis." *Number 31328.* 4th edition. Athens: John D. Kollarou & Company, 1959, pp. 10–11. A member of the Royal Belgian Academy, Liebrecht explains the universal appeal of *Number 31328* on the grounds that many peoples during the Second World War also knew what it meant to be enslaved by a greater power.

LOUKAS, STRATIS. *Story of a Captive.* Athens: John D. Kollarou & Company, 1929. Along with *Number 31328,* this novel evokes the experience suffered by those who were taken for the labor battalions after the Catastrophe of 1922.

PANAYOTOPOULOS, I. M. *Writers and Their Works.* II. Athens: Eagle Editions, 1943. A general commentary on language and its use in prose writing introduces a series of essays on twenty-one Greek authors of the 'thirties and 'forties. The essays are biographical and describe some of the works.

SAHINIS, APOSTOLOS. "The Fiction of Elias Venezis," Tr. by Gabriel Drachman. *The Charioteer,* I (Autumn, 1960), pp. 84–90. In this brief article the author sketches some of the important characters in the novels of Venezis.

SIKELIANOS, ANGHELOS. "Prologue of Anghelos Sikelianos for the Second Edition of Beyond the Aegean." *Beyond the Aegean.* 6th edition. Athens: John D. Kollarou & Company, 1965, pp. 9–13. One of Greece's greatest modern poets writes an extended tribute to *Beyond the Aegean.*

STAVRIANOS, L. S. *Greece: American Dilemma and Opportunity.* Chicago: Henry Regnery Company, 1952. A leading historian of the Balkans details the tragic events of the Second World War and afterwards. A reading of the volume places in perspective the background of Venezis' own writings inspired by the conflict.

VALETAS, G. *Anthology of Demotic Prose Writers,* III. 1888–1922. Athens: Petros Panos, 1949. The editor has compiled a valuable collection of writings for the period covered by his anthology. Of interest to the student is the section devoted to the "Aeolian School" to which Venezis belongs. Reprinted are two short selections from *Number 31328* and *Beyond the Aegean.*

Index